The Book of Opals

Plate 1: A breathtaking gem of the finest quality. Black opal surrounded by 17 flawless marquise diamonds. The piece is valued at $50,000. (Photo courtesy of W. H. Walker.)

THE BOOK OF
OPALS

WILFRED CHARLES EYLES

CHARLES E. TUTTLE COMPANY
Rutland, Vermont & Tokyo, Japan

Representatives:

For Continental Europe:
BOXERBOOKS, INC., Zurich

For the British Isles:
PRENTICE-HALL INTERNATIONAL, INC., London

For Canada:
HURTIG PUBLISHERS, Edmonton

For Australasia:
BOOK WISE (AUSTRALIA) PTY. LTD.
104–108 Sussex Street, Sydney 2000

Published by the Charles E. Tuttle Company, Inc.
of Rutland, Vermont & Tokyo, Japan
with editorial offices at
Suido 1-chome, 2-6, Bunkyo-ku, Tokyo

Copyright in Japan, 1964
by Charles E. Tuttle Company, Inc.

All rights reserved

Library of Congress Catalog
Card No. 64–14193

International Standard Book No. 0-8048-0068-5

First printing, 1964
Seventh printing, 1976

Layout of illustrations by S. Katakura
Book design and typography by Kaoru Ogimi
PRINTED IN JAPAN

Table of Contents

	List of Illustrations	9
	Foreword *by Lelande Quick*	11
	Preface	13
	Acknowledgment	17
1.	Opal	23
2.	The Color in Opals	35
3.	Opal Types and Colors	48
4.	White Cliffs	57
5.	Queensland	65
6.	The Eulo Queen	72
7.	Lightning Ridge	75
8.	Andamooka	98
9.	Coober Pedy and Tintinbar	111
10.	Rainbow Ridge	118
11.	Querétaro and Some Minor Localities	134
12.	The Opal Trade	140
13.	Superstitions Regarding Opals	152
14.	The Preservation of Opals	156
15.	Equipment for Gem Production	158
16.	The Cutting of the Gem	164
17.	The Doublet or Two-Piece Opal	168
18.	Some Opal Peculiarities	172
19.	On to Lightning Ridge	176
20.	Australian Journeys	185
21.	Wollaston's Journey for Opal	190
22.	In Conclusion	212
	Glossary	217
	Index	221

List of Illustrations

Figures

1.	Map of Australian Opal Fields	58
2.	Typical Shaft Structure at Lightning Ridge	82
3.	Geological Map of the Andamooka Opal Field	100
4.	Geological Stratification at Andamooka	103
5.	Road Map of Northwest Nevada (Rainbow Ridge)	120
6.	Map of Rainbow Ridge Opal Mine	121
7.	Map of Mexico and Central America	135
8.	Map of the Opal Fields of Honduras	138

Plates

1 (Frontispiece).	Black opal surrounded by 17 marquise diamonds	4
2.	Large uncut opal from Andamooka	27
3.	"The Big Opal," largest ever mined in Nevada	28
4.	Specimen of common opal, Nevada	28
5.	Rough specimens from Andamooka	29
6.	Rough opals and cut gems from Australian fields	30
7.	Grand opal mounted with six two-carat diamonds, Andamooka	39
8.	Large rough specimen	40
9.	Rough opal specimen, Rainbow Ridge	40
10.	Mexican cherry and honey opal, Querétaro	49
11.	Cut and polished black opal, Rainbow Ridge	49
12.	Opalized shells from South Australia	50
13.	Large opal specimen with mosaic inlays, Andamooka	51
14.	Collection of mounted opals (black opals, blue opal, and pin-fire opal), Coober Pedy	52
15.	Miner's shanty, Lightning Ridge	77
16.	Main Street, Lightning Ridge	77

List of Illustrations

17.	View of mine dumps, Lightning Ridge	78
18.	Typical residence at Lightning Ridge	79
19.	Main Street, Walgett, New South Wales	79
20.	The train to Walgett	80
21.	Truck service from Walgett to Lightning Ridge	80
22.	Large uncut specimen of opal, Andamooka	105
23.	Rough uncut specimens of opal, Andamooka	106
24.	Miners' establishments at Coober Pedy	115
25.	The owner of Rainbow Ridge working a drift	125
26.	The main tunnel, Rainbow Ridge	125
27.	The wall rock with encrusted opals, Rainbow Ridge	126
28.	Keith Hodson mining at Rainbow Ridge	126
29.	Outstanding black opal mounted as a pendant	143
30.	Rare black opal gem	144
31.	Black opal with coal-red fire flashing	145
32.	Opal bracelet from Australian opal	146
33.	Compact gem saw	159
34.	Grinding wheel with sander and polishing disc on end	159
35.	12-inch cast iron lap	160
36.	8-inch polishing disc	160
37.	Light-duty drill press	161
38.	Assorted tools used in gem production	161
39.	High speed hand tool with saws, bits, grinders, etc.	162
40.	The Kite brothers at their camp, Lightning Ridge	179
41.	The Kite brothers by one of their shafts	180

Foreword

IT IS indeed timely, when the interest in the world runs higher than ever before in the opal, the most beautiful of all the precious stones, that my old friend Wilfred C. Eyles should write the most comprehensive book on the opal that has yet been written in North America. There is probably no one who has been to as many of the world's opal fields, as a buyer and a miner, or who has dealt in opals longer than Mr. Eyles. Certainly there is no one who loves them more.

Many years ago Mr. Eyles invented the diamond saw, which performed for the oldest art of gem cutting what the invention of the gasoline engine did for transportation. More than anything else, it was responsible for the tremendous growth of the amateur lapidary movement in North America, where gem cutting has become the fastest-growing of leisure-time craft hobbies. The favorite gem of millions of amateur gem cutters, the opal has been in wide demand among them, and the supply has been depleting rapidly. The demand daily grows greater, and now, with the building of large middle-class groups of people in Europe and Japan, the opal is in great demand in the world jewelry trade.

The leading commercial supply is at several locations in Australia, all described in this book. The locations were about depleted and abandoned when Mr. Eyles began to write this account, but modern methods, such as surface stripping with bulldozers, revived most of the mining locations. Late in 1962 it was reported that through the use of modern core drilling methods many new locations were being discovered and many deposits were found beneath the workings in old mines earlier believed exhausted. The result is that many of the nearly deserted mines now have hundreds of miners busily engaged in unearthing new supplies of opal that still cannot fill the wide demand of the Japanese, American, and German cutters.

The opal is the only one of the so-called precious stones that has never been successfully imitated or synthesized, and it is safe from imitation until the real cause of fire and other colors in opal is actually determined. Many unproved theories exist as to the cause of the changing colors in opal, but until someone can duplicate the correct process no theory can ever be accepted.

Opal has been a favorite gem stone throughout the world longer than any other, and all lovers of gems will indeed profit by a reading of Mr. Eyles's good account of it.

Lelande Quick
founder of the *Lapidary Journal*

Preface

THE AUTHOR of this book, who has been for many years a professional mineralogist and an accomplished lapidary, has made a special study of opal. This interesting gem has held an attraction for him, as it has for a great many other people, based not only on its great beauty but also on its other characteristics, which the reader will discover as he proceeds with this work.

In the author's later years, he has dealt with no other gem stone but opal, visiting opal fields and mining the gem at various Australian locations and at its only source in the United States: Rainbow Ridge in the state of Nevada. Between 1953 and 1956, he made four trips to his native land, Australia, where he visited a number of opal fields and purchased opal for his present trade, that of opal dealer. On these trips he met miners in the field, observed their methods of mining, and studied their way of life, at the same time studying the geology and the formations of the fields. These fields, incidentally, have produced a great amount of revenue, not only for the miners and the trade but for the Australian economy as well. Also during his visits to Australia opal dealers and cutters were contacted, and opal was purchased. Much was learned of the dealers' methods of trade and of the operating techniques of the various cutters, who were found to be very efficient in their profession.

Before attempting to write this work on opal, the author devoted much study to the subject. In the past he had many good friends who wrote articles on opal; many of these articles he found to be well written but concerned only with some single aspect of the gem. He believed, however, that anyone who wished to write fully on the subject should not only have had scientific laboratory experience but should also have been a cutter of the gem, and a miner of it as well —this so as to have been able to observe the various peculiarities of this interesting and alluring stone in its natural formations.

It is indeed very doubtful that any other gem stone in existence could be a subject for any extensive research. We have diamonds, emeralds, rubies, topazes, etc., but what is there to cover of any great amount of interest, outside of their locations, their varieties, and their position in the jewelry business?

As the reader progresses, he will readily observe that opal is without doubt, without contradiction, probably the world's most interesting gem stone. The reader will also note that despite the scientific studies made of opal over the years, there still exist many many unexplainable mysteries that remain to be solved. It was while taking up some of these peculiarities of the gem with my good friend Dr. H. C. Dake, editor of the *Mineralogist* and an outstanding authority on opal himself, that it was suggested that I should cover the subject in a book, outlining its various historical backgrounds and covering the subject in its entirety—something which seems to have been either overlooked or somehow or other never before fully elaborated upon. The author, in covering the subject, will try to make the reading not only interesting but also educational.

An interesting feature that he would like to bring to the attention of the reader is that it is hardly possible for him to realize the terrible hardships endured by the early-day prospectors who were in the main responsible for the discovery of opal in Australia. These hardships were far greater than prospectors in the early days encountered in the wide open spaces of the United States. The vast regions of central Australia are even today much the same as they were in Tully Wollaston's time. In this "outback" area, as it is called, one can stand on an ant hill and peer off to the horizon, whose heat appears like that of a furnace.

No wonder this "outback" is also called the Never-Never, a very appropriate name. The awful loneliness is hard to imagine, for no other place in the world is as lonely as this Never-Never. On the American deserts there are always numerous mountain ranges within a reasonable distance. In Alaska one can obtain some companionship in the never-ending scenery of mountains, lakes, and forests. But in this outback of central Australia there is not one single thing to break the monotony. Today there is no outback left in the wide open spaces of the United States. Good roads and transportation have eliminated it. Another difference between the two regions is that water is never far distant in the United States, whereas in Australia it is very scarce. Rainfall during the summer months from thunderstorms is rather common in the United States. But in the outback of Australia, even now at the Andamooka and Coober Pedy opal field areas, the annual rainfall is only about five inches. From South Australia to the west, across the Nullabar Plains, travels the Trans-Australian Railroad. This railroad traverses the longest straight section of line in the world, over three hundred miles without any variation, and as level as a billiard table.

In those early days, prospectors, explorers, and adventurers were also attacked by unfriendly blacks (aboriginals), and no one will ever know how many were killed, how many died of thirst, or how many went mad from the awful monotony of the loneliness. With knowledge of these conditions the reader can envision the extreme hardships that were endured by these early-day prospectors who first discovered opal.

This work is dedicated to those hardy, courageous souls who, with their unlimited endurance and perseverance, stumbled on and on to discover opal at last. Few ever gained any financial rewards, but it would seem to have been their destiny to enhance the gem world with their discovery of the most mysterious, colorful, and enchanting of all gem stones.

Acknowledgment

GRATEFUL acknowledgment is made to the following persons who, in one way or another, were of valuable assistance to the author in the writing of this book.

The late Mr. Lelande Quick, founder and former editor of the *Lapidary Journal*, who wrote the foreword.

Dr. Henry C. Dake, former editor of the *Mineralogist* and nationally noted authority not only on opal but on all gems and minerals, whose advice and suggestions in relation to the book are deeply appreciated.

The late Mr. William Burton Pitts, outstanding gem authority, dean of American lapidaries, and honorary gem curator at the Academy of Sciences, San Francisco, California, who gave the author his earliest instructions in the lapidary arts.

Dr. George Switzer, curator of mineralogy at the Smithsonian Institution, the United States National Museum, who advised on opal in Honduras.

The late Mr. John Melhase, famous mineral collector of Berkeley, California, geologist for the Southern Pacific Railroad, and first president of the Northern California Mineral and Gem Society, who was the author's companion on many field trips to the Rainbow Ridge mine.

Señor Pedro Gonzales, well-known opal miner and dealer of Querétaro, Mexico, who served as the author's companion and guide in Mexico.

Mr. E. Gregory Sherman, largest buyer of opal in the various fields of production and world-wide dealer in opal, who has for some years provided the author with much fine opal.

Acknowledgment

The late Dr. Austin Flint Rogers, professor emeritus of mineralogy at Leland Stanford University and friend of long standing, who had a never-ending addiction to research, especially in relation to colors in opal.

The Kite brothers: Luke, Shirl, Bill, and Foley, miners at the Nine Mile, Lightning Ridge, whose kindness and entertainment during the author's residence at the Ridge are remembered with gratitude.

Mr. G. F. Claringbull, curator of mineralogy, British Museum, London, who supplied information on opal in Honduras.

Mr. Henry Symonds, curator and statistician, California State Division of Mines, who was instrumental in providing the author with considerable data on various common opal deposits in California.

The late Mr. Edward Murphy, esteemed gentleman and renowned buyer, whom the author met during the first world war on a visit to Australia and who provided considerable data on various episodes of the early days at White Cliffs, Wilcannia, and Lightning Ridge.

Mr. Keith Hodson, present-day owner and operator of the Rainbow Ridge mine, whose permission to use the mine's photographs is appreciated.

Mr. Mark Foster, prospector, miner, and early-day caretaker at the Rainbow Ridge mine and friend of the author, with whom he mined many times at Rainbow Ridge.

The late Mrs. F. H. Lockheed, famous woman of her day and early-day operator and developer of the Rainbow Ridge mine, who gave the author much of its early history.

Messrs. Cherney and Altman, prominent opal dealers of Melbourne, Australia, who kindly offered the use of their photographs.

Mr. and Mrs. Dan Archevelita, operators of the now extinct Virgin Ranch in Virgin Valley Nevada, who befriended the author on visits in early days and who grub-staked many down-and-out and penniless miners of the day.

Mr. Earl W. Shaw, outstanding desert prospector of Yermo, California, whom the author accompanied on dozens of explorations throughout the western United States—the Mojave Desert, Death Valley, the Funeral Mountains, etc. —where common opal was, in most places, found in abundance.

Mr. Francis S. Sperisen, nationally known professional lapidary of San Francisco and author of *The Art of the Lapidary,* who over many years has given the author considerable advice relating to the lapidary art.

The Australian Bulletin, which has permitted use of the article entitled "When the Tank Dries Up" (November 4, 1961).

The South Australian Department of Geology, which has provided considerable data on the geology of the Andamooka and the Coober Pedy opal fields.

Miss Vivian Killian, of San Francisco and the University of California, who served as my proofreader and, with subject matter strange and foreign to her, accomplished a most praiseworthy job with the manuscript.

The Book of Opals

Ask God why He made the gem so small
   And so huge granite.
Because God meant that man,
   Should place a higher value on it.

                              ROBERT BURNS

1 Opal

OPAL IS without doubt the world's most colorful gem stone. No other precious gem produces the array of beautiful colors that it does. Mineralogically speaking, opal is a silicate, its chemical composition being SiO_2H_2O. It has a varied hardness of from 5 to $6\frac{1}{2}$; it is brittle and has an uneven and sometimes conchoidal fracture. Its hues are many, ranging from colorless to every color in the spectrum. It also contains all the intermediate colors as well, and those opals that contain a variety of colors are always in great demand for their gem values.

The mineral common opal, which has practically no value, is widely distributed throughout the world. It is very easily distinguished from the other silica minerals by its limpid appearance as well as its greasy luster. Some of this common opal is very highly fluorescent under ultraviolet light, giving off a good color which is usually green.

Opal has a specific gravity of from 2.0 to 2.1. It has single refraction and a refractive index between 1.45 and 1.46. It is noncrystalline or, in other words, amorphous. Under the polarized microscope, we obtain the identical results with glass and obsidian, both also being amorphous. Some authorities believe that certain types of opal show a microcrystalline structure; this could be very possible, for there is no doubt that quartz pseudomorphs after opal exist, and where they may exist, this changeover is impossible to detect.

The formula changing over from SiO_2H_2O to SiO_2 certainly is feasible, and opal showing any crystalline structure could be undergoing metamorphic changeover. Silica, the constituent of opal, is also the basic mineral in quartz, sand, jasper, flint, quartz crystal, and a host of other common minerals and semiprecious stones.

In opal, the silica is combined with a water content of as much, in some cases, as ten percent. The final mixture is a kind of hard jelly of the silica and water. It may form a paper-thin lining in or on porous basaltic rocks of igneous origin. It may occur in lumps or nodules. A precious type may be a nodule no larger than an almond nut and may have the same identical shape, especially if it is from the Lightning Ridge field, in which case it is in a definite formation of clays.

In the earliest days of opal history, the stones were mined first at Csermenitsa in Hungary. It was not until modern times that new fields were discovered in Australia. The first Australian discovery was at White Cliffs in the state of New South Wales. A few years later another extensive area was found in the state of Queensland. In the New World, precious opal has been mined in Mexico at Querétaro and in the state of Nevada, U. S. A., at a place about 40 miles south of the small outpost of Denio on the Oregon border. Here is the famous Rainbow Ridge mine, where grand specimens of opal have been discovered.

It has been stated that opal has been mined in Honduras. This I tend to doubt; however, if it is so, then it has been only in a small localized instance, for there is no record of any commercial production of any size. To verify this, I consulted Dr. George Switzer, curator of mineralogy at the Smithsonian Institution. Dr. Switzer replied that the Smithsonian Institution did have two small specimens that were supposed to be from Honduras, adding that these were not on exhibit. From this assertion I gained the impression that these opals were either of doubtful origin or not of sufficient quality to be placed on exhibit. I shall have more to say about Honduran opal in a later chapter.

Common opal, unlike the gem or precious opal, almost always consists of a definite solid color: red, brown, blue, or green. The last of these is sometimes referred to as prase opal. Precious opal is rare in the gem world. Although it is still obtainable, it is far from being as plentiful or as common as diamonds, which many people consider to be as rare. This is not the case, for diamonds are controlled by a cartel or trust and only dispensed as the market demands. If diamonds were dispensed without control, they would probably flood our dime stores. Precious opal has never been that common, and its market has never been controlled.

Common opal, when activated by ultraviolet light, will usually show excellent fluorescence. This is usually prized by mineral collectors. Precious opals display a great variety of colors — every color of the spectrum, some claim. It will be found that they reveal every intermediate color also. It would be impossible for anyone to designate all the various colors that a selection of precious opals displays.

The jewelry trade is responsible for the various names given to color types of precious opal: names such as Harlequin opal, fire opal, pin-fire opal, and of course black opal, the last always commanding higher prices. The so-called black opals are from one field—Lightning Ridge—and this field produces opals mainly of all-dark-base opal, which are not necessarily black, since some are blue, red, and other colors. They are almost always associated with a dark-gray potch (common opal). Sometimes the opal colors permeate this potch. The so-called Harlequin opal is a type containing many varied colors and shows a multitude of miniature tile-like formations on the surface of the stone. Pin-fire opal is a type in which the main body of the stone is usually white and shows a myriad of small pinlike colors all through the surface and the body of the stone.

I have observed hundreds of opals from Lightning Ridge and have yet to find one that could really be termed black, as we know the color of black to be. At Rainbow Ridge I mined much opal, and a jet-black common opal was always much in evidence; in fact, it could easily be mistaken for obsidian.

A student of mineralogy attempting to identify a specimen of this black opal from Rainbow Ridge could very easily be misled. In most cases his decision would be that it was obsidian, regardless of what tests were given for color, fracture, hardness, or specific gravity, none being conclusive. The only test that distinguishes the two definitely is the crushing of a sample, which is then placed in a test tube and held over a Bunsen burner in order to obtain the vapor of the existing water.

All opal contains water in its composition. This ranges from two percent to as much as ten percent, depending mainly upon the locality from which it is derived. Opal at Rainbow Ridge contains a very high percentage of water; opal from the Australian fields, a much lesser amount. It is mainly for this reason that Australian opals are more durable and suitable as gems.

At Querétaro, Mexico, some fine opals which are embedded in a very hard igneous rock (rhyolite) are mined. Many opals are ruined in the attempt to extract the gem material from this rock. Querétaro also produces a very fine honey-colored opal that is attractive and contains little of any other color.

Hyalite opal is a glass-clear variety and is almost always found in the coating or filling of vugs of basaltic igneous rocks. Sometimes this opal is found in botryoidal form.

Most opals can be readily determined, since the stones

differ enormously from field to field. For instance, no white milk opals are found at Lightning Ridge. The darker-base opal which is found at Lightning Ridge is not found at Andamooka or Coober Pedy. Opal found in the state of Queensland is associated with a hard limonite mineral locally called ironstone. This type of opal is not found in the other Australian fields. The opal from Rainbow Ridge in Nevada can usually be identified by the crazing or spider-web fracturing in or on the surface of the material. The opal from Querétaro, Mexico, can readily be distinguished by the rhyolite matrix which is usually associated with the gem material.

Some authorities have elaborated upon opal in such a manner that the uninitiated could very easily be misled into believing that opal is to be found in abundance in a great many places. This is far from the truth. These authorities have included the mineral (common) opal in their reports. There is a world of difference between the gem variety and the common opal. It is true that common opal is found in abundance and has practically no value, either as a mineral or as a gem source. Much has been written from time to time of many opal locations in various parts of the world, including those in the United States. When these locations are checked, they mainly prove to contain common opal, the authors making no distinction between this common variety and gem opal.

I am acquainted with a deposit of this common opal about five miles northeast of the small town of Milford, Utah. This deposit covers several square acres and descends from the surface to a depth of five or six feet. It is composed entirely of common opal of a great many varied colors. No commercial use of it has ever been obtained, although some enterprising individuals have tried to introduce and market it to the building trade; however, it was found to be too brittle for any use. Even with such a huge deposit as this, situated in a sedimentary intrusion containing volcanic ash, not a single speck of gem opal has ever been found.

The California State Division of Mines, where I once worked as assistant technologist, lists over fifty localities in the state where opal exists. Bulletins issued by the State Division of Mines give these exact locations. In the neighboring state of Nevada, about twenty miles north of Gabbs and close to Highway 23, I mined out a considerable quantity of large and colorful opalized logs (opal pseudomorph after wood). Also in the same state, in the vicinity of Tonopah, there exists much common opal. Forty miles west of Tonopah, in the vicinity of Coaldale, common opal is plentiful. Collectors venturing out into these desert areas should always make inquiries at local gasoline stations, for only a very sparse population inhabits this desert country. The states of Oregon, Idaho, and Arizona all have many areas where common opal exists.

The state of California has been credited with having precious opal, the reason being that a few isolated small chips were found some years ago in basalt in Red Rock Canyon, Kern County, and at Zabriskie Point close by the small township of Shoshone, in Inyo County. Here pinpoints of color permeate a dehydrated clay, which crumbles easily when handled. No material of a gem nature has ever been found in either place, and there is not a single specimen on display in the elaborate State Mineral Museum located in the Ferry Building in San Francisco.

Some years ago, I was acquainted with a well-known mineral man and prospector from Nampa, Idaho, who had discovered a few very small gemmy fragments extracted from vugs in the local basalt. Immediately the reports were exaggerated to the extent that it would seem another Lightning Ridge had been discovered. Time proved that these few fragments were the entire extent of the discovery.

It is generally known by mineralogists that isolated discoveries of an odd gemmy fragment of opal have occurred, mainly in some igneous-rock location. It may be mentioned that, geologically speaking, the occurrence of gem opal in any quantity in igneous rocks is as a rule very rare, Querétaro being the one exception and the only place in the world where gem opal in igneous rock in any quantity exists. This opal is not in basalt but is rather a filling of the vugs in rhyolite. Opal at Lightning Ridge, Andamooka, and Coober Pedy, Australia, is all in a sedimentary zone, where no igneous rocks exist.

It is known that some gem opal was produced in early times in Hungary and what is now known as eastern Ceskoslovensko. It has been stated that these mines were worked as long as 2,000 years ago. However, the opal produced here in the early nineteenth century was of a rather poor quality; that is, poor in comparison with gem opal from present productive areas. No opal has been produced from this locality since approximately 1930. It is extremely doubtful that opal of any great amount with which to furnish the gem trade in general was ever produced. Proof of this lies in the fact that when Tully Wollaston arrived in London, in 1889, with some outstanding opal from various Queensland localities, the gem merchants of Covent Garden had evidently never before seen gem opal. They even termed his opal an imitation and a fake and refused to accept or buy it. Covent Garden was considered the world's center for the gem trade at the time. This we know for a fact; if any gem opal was produced in any commercial quantity, why were these high-class gem merchants so ignorant of Wollaston's opal?

Some opals have appeared in such places as Egypt, India, and also Japan. In early times, these places, with some others, have been given some credit for its origin. Opal had no doubt, in all these cases, been carried from the early Hungarian source, for there is no record of any gem opal originating in these lands.

There are authentic records made by various archeologists that such gems as lapis lazuli, said to have been the favorite jewel of Cleopatra, have been unearthed in Egypt. Jade artifacts valued by the Incas and the Aztecs were excavated in Mexico and some other Latin American countries, but with all the disclosures made by archeologists in Greece, Rome, Egypt, and Mexico, not a single opal has been discovered. All of which proves that although the ancients had many of the other gems, opal was unknown.

Therefore the reader can discount the majority of locations given for gem-quality opal. He can content himself that outside of the various Australian fields and those of Querétaro, Mexico, and Nevada in the United States, no others of any consequence exist.

2 The Color in Opals

IN REFERENCE to color, it is important that one should have some knowledge of just what color really is, in order to be able to understand the nature of the colors in opal.

Color is the result of a collision, and a collision cannot occur unless at least one of the parties is traveling. The traveler here is light, the fastest of all speeders. Most of our light, of course, comes from the sun across some 93 million miles of empty space. It is part of the radiant energy poured forth by that star day and night in all directions. The journey to the earth takes about eight minutes, and on the way the speeding light meets no obstacles. Out in space it is colorless light. When it collides with myriads of different surfaces on the face of the earth, this colorless light reveals the various colors of the rainbow.

Obviously then, these radiant colors must have been somehow hidden in the light of outer space. When this light strikes a surface, something must happen to reveal them. We can only explain this by the nature of the light itself. First, it fans out from its source in straight lines in all directions. Second, it travels out in tiny pulses of energy. There are many different wave lengths in a beam of light. At the normal speed of light, all these wave lengths are blended together. We can think of each wave length as a thread and of a beam of white light as being made of many threads. When a sunbeam strikes a surface, the skein of threads is broken apart. Some are absorbed by the object. The rest are reflected back to our eyes to see. And we see them as colors.

The basic colors of the spectrum are red, orange, yellow, green, indigo, and violet. However, there are countless half tones and tinges between the basic colors. The red rays have the longest wave lengths, the orange have shorter wave lengths, and so on down to the violet, which have the shortest wave lengths.

When a beam of light strikes a red rose, all the orange, green, and blue rays are absorbed. The red rays are bounced back for our eyes to see. When a sunbeam falls upon the wings of a bluebird, all the red, orange, yellow, and green rays are absorbed, and the blues are reflected back. When the sun shines on a piece of polished ebony (black), all the rays are absorbed, and none are reflected back. When a sunbeam strikes a calla lily (white), none of the rays are absorbed, and the light is reflected back in its natural whiteness.

Over the many years that I have been engaged in the science of both mineralogy and gemmology, I have many times encountered the question: How do we account for the colors in opal? The science of chemistry has determined the colors of every other gem stone, but opal has so far defied it.

The first time I encountered the subject, I was in the company of the late John Melhase, a fine gentleman and a noted mineral collector, as well as the geologist for the Southern Pacific Railroad. He was usually my field-trip companion. The time I speak of was 1934, when I was working at the California State Division of Mines as assistant technician to the late Frank Sanborn, whom the mineral Sanbornite is named after. The Southern Pacific Building being a stone's throw from the Ferry Building, where the Division of Mines is situated in San Francisco, it was my daily custom to have lunch with John Melhase, and in the course of time we began to take our holidays together. On one of these holidays we decided we should visit the opal field at Rainbow Ridge, Nevada. Both of us had visited the place in former times, and we thought it appropriate to write to the caretaker, Mr. Mark Foster, to inform him of our impending visit. The roads to the area in those days were very similar to those now existing at Andamooka and Coober Pedy in South Australia. They were rough indeed, and very few travelers ever had occasion to travel that route. Cars also were not too fast, but they were sturdy characters.

In due time we arrived early one evening and found Mark awaiting us; we also found that he had another guest on the field: one of our long-time friends, Mr. Charlie Barnett of Portland, Oregon. Charlie secretly informed us that Mark had received our letter and had remarked that he was expecting a couple of high-hat brain trusters. Advised of this remark, we knew exactly how to act accordingly, and we were treated with the utmost courtesy after getting acquainted. The next day we all four went into the mine tunnel to mine out opal. Working all day, we obtained our share of opal.

In the evening, discussing things in general with regard to mining, which naturally is the custom under such circumstances, I asked Mark whether anyone had ever suggested the source from which the colors were derived. I received my answer, and it was one which I have never forgotten. Mark, a dyed-in-the-wool desert rat with an obvious background of much learning gained somewhere in the past, said: "Almost all theories advanced have come from men working in a laboratory, who have never mined or cut any opal."

Of course we did not think he was referring to either myself or Melhase. He evidently had in mind some other authorities, whoever they may have been. From that time on, over the years, I have delved into the subject and consulted a great many expert authorities. I questioned the curators in Australian museums, as well as many in the

United States, among whom were men such as the late Dr. Austin Flint Rogers, professor emeritus of mineralogy at Stanford University. Dr. Rogers was a noted scientist who was always greatly interested in unsolved problems, such as the explanation for the color in opal. He observed that the various lines of thought regarding these colors were theories only. I had many times consulted my good friend, Mr. Francis S. Sperisen, who certainly could be termed an authority, being one of the foremost professional lapidaries and gemmologists in the nation, and the author of the book, *The Art of the Lapidary*. Mr. Sperisen, after being shown a great many varied subject specimens containing combinations of color, had no answer concerning the problem.

Another well-known national figure is Dr. H. C. Dake, noted editor of the *Mineralogist*, a magazine that has been published for many years in the city of Portland, Oregon. Dr. Dake has for a great many years given every aspect of the subject much study. He has, during the long period of his editorship, encountered every theory that has been advanced regarding these colors, and he should be considered an authority of distinction. In his recent correspondence to me, he states: "It is quite problematic whether opal will ever be synthesized in the laboratory in any successful manner. A good deal of work is now being done in the laboratory on this gem. This is not generally known. The rewards would of course be very considerable to anyone perfecting a really successful duplicate."

While no specific information has been given at this time, it is understood that one of the most promising methods is the use of high-frequency "vibrations" of some type on common opal. In short, the idea seems to be to try to convert a good deal of solid-mass common opal into the precious type. Theoretically this is quite possible. This method represents only one school of thought and is only an experiment.

Plate 7: A grand opal of sky blue and sunset colors, mounted with six diamonds of two carats each. From Andamooka. (Photo courtesy of W. H. Walker.)

Plate 8: Cross-section of large uncut opal mined by Mr. Glen Hodson, owner and operator of the Rainbow Ridge Mine, Nevada.

Plate 9: Beautiful rough opal specimen from the Rainbow Ridge Mine, Nevada. It is encased in a cylindrical container. Courtesy of Glen Hodson, owner and operator of the mine.

Another school of thought involves working on the old silica-gel idea. The experimenters allow the mass to set or partly set and then try to introduce the "microscopic" fractures or whatever they suspect may be the cause of the spectral colors in the opal. This method is also theoretically possible.

As should be known, opal stands alone in the world today in that it is the last remaining gem that has absolutely no imitation in any remotely passable form. This seems unique, but rarely have we seen any mention of it in print. In short, even a layman knowing nothing about gems can very easily distinguish the difference between the genuine and the counterfeit opal, but this is not so with the other man-made gem imitations. Of course it may be that if enough research and experimentation is done, then opal could also eventually be "made." Personally I am not so confident that this situation will ever occur. As all my scientific friends and I point out, since the reasons for the colors are not definitely known, it is much harder to attack the problem. So opal may be defiant for a long time to come.

A fact that may or may not be significant is that in every case where a reddish film coats some rough opals on a contact zone this opal reveals very flashy fire colors. This coating is not to be confused with matrix. It definitely appears to be an iron-film staining; however, in these cases the rough opal never shows any colors other than red.

During the many years of study regarding these colors in opal, several theories have been advanced, but, as previously stated, they are theories only. No proof has ever been established to substantiate them. And anyone who is acquainted with any science will not accept an unproven theory, since it is worth little until it is proved.

In most cases where these theories have been advanced, they are, if not absolutely disproven, then exceedingly doubtful. For instance, one widely circulated theory concerning the colors in opal was that, because opal always contains a variable amount of water, possibly the reflection of light by the water molecules was the cause of the colors. If this were so, however, how could we account for the fact that a great amount of opal shows absolutely no play of color at all, while much opal displays an extraordinary range of colors?

Of course we have this situation with quartz also. We have clear quartz and colored quartz "amethyst," and both are the same; but we know that the source of the color in "amethyst" is the manganese. Another theory that has been advanced is that reflected light on a series of built-up parallel layers disperses the colors, but while it is true that some varieties of precious opals do show parallel lines of color, they do not show any built-up structures. We have observed in some specimens of opal that these lines were not always the same. Some would have a color line of a "definite" color, such as red, green, and in some cases blue. These colors were not distributed throughout the opal but were definite color lines only.

Another theory given wide circulation was that the play of color was similar to the Newton colors, or to the colors of an oil slick upon water, which all of us have observed at one time or other. It is quite true that certain types of precious opal do give this impression, but again this does not hold true in general at all. For a great many specimens of opal found on the fields, especially Australian fields, are neither clear nor translucent but rather opaque, and, regardless of any orientation, they show one solid color only, which is sometimes green, sometimes blue, and sometimes even lavender.

How do we explain the fact that this opaque opal is of a single solid color? What is the reason for the impurity of this color? At present there is no answer. We may add here that the various colors in opal are far greater than the colors of the spectrum. It is doubtful that anyone could enumerate these colors, for not only are all the primary colors obtained but also all the secondary and intermediate colors exist.

For instance, I observed at the Rainbow Ridge mine in Nevada, where I mined in the drifts by the light of the lamp hanging at the rear, that as I dug out clefts of the hard-packed clay, a vivid flash of color would sometimes be in evidence; then alongside this would be a piece of absolutely water-clear opal. Why would this piece alongside a beautifully colorful piece be clear, with no color whatever? At times great quantities of opal mined here proved to have a cloudy citrine color, and at times I would obtain a great many pieces that were jet black and resembled obsidian. I also obtained white, opaque milk opal very similar to that from Andamooka, South Australia. This jet-black opal intrigued me, since black in minerals is usually carbon, manganese, etc. What is the color pigment of this black opal? Neither optics nor chemistry, each with its definite tests of determination, has thus far been able to provide an answer to this question.

Another theory dealing with this problem has suggested that the play of colors in opal is probably due to the effects of multitudinous planes of material, each having a slightly different refractive index from the material adjacent to it, and that the planes, being striated with microscopic lines and producing diffraction of light from these lines, play their part in the production of the various colors. This concept claims that the play of colors due to the ordinary partial absorption of white light could be gleams of almost pure spectrum colors composed of narrow bands of wave lengths, such as are seen in a rainbow or a glass prism.

Spectrographic examination shows that the colors of opal are highly monochromatic; that is, the light is of a single wave length. This has been thought to result in opal from the spacing of the silica films, which produce intense color reflections, and the regulation of the wave length of light so that only a small band is visible if viewed through the spectroscope, the film spacing being harmonic of the color produced. Where there are numbers of sheets, one behind the other, they then strengthen the color as long as they are also of a closely related spacing. This wave-length idea, being similar to that of tuning in a certain wave length on the radio to obtain a given station or frequency, sounds reasonable in regard to some varieties of opal. But, as I have pointed out, there are many more colors in opal than exist in a prism, a rainbow, or the Newton colors of the spectrum.

I have made thin sections of opal which contained very beautiful colors at one end of the section and were absolutely devoid of any color at the other end. What happened here? Why were the beautiful colors displayed only at one end and not at the other end of the section? Everything else was equal. Then again, if the above optical theory held water, this disappearance of color should not have been evident.

If one were to make a study of the many varieties of opal, using hundreds of pieces, one would find that no two pieces are identical. Some would be of the jelly type, some with mixed colors, some with colored parallel lines running throughout the piece, some opaque and with a definite permanent color. Many pieces, especially the precious types, would, on orientation, display other colors. All this is very confusing, and it has for many years defied science to arrive at any solution. I have also made thin sections of precious opal which, when viewed with magnification, were seen to be absolutely colorless. Then again, a given thin section—thin as half a millimeter—will sometimes show a fine color effect on one side which is much superior to that of the opposite side. This clearly shows that, even in such a thin section, the colors do not always permeate the piece.

Opal, for instance, from Querétaro, Mexico, showing a beautiful display of color equal to that of some other opals, when cut thin and backed with black will often show to no advantage, whereas the same thin section of opal from the Australian fields will reveal beautiful colors. It is these thin sections of Australian opal backed on the bottom by black that go to make the beautiful doublets used in jewelry. This effect is impossible to obtain from any other opal. Why is this? Thus far there is no answer.

Some observers at times have compared the colors sometimes found in quartz crystals to those found in opal and have thought that they were similar. These colors are of a prismatic nature and have absolutely no relation whatever to those in opal. It is definitely known that they are caused by internal stress or in some cases by fractures in the crystal. Then again, they are only primary colors, and opal displays many more colors than the primary ones.

Some observers have also remarked that the colors in opal are similar to those of the rainbow, but again these colors are of the spectrum, and opal, as I have pointed out, in many cases has solid colors, as well as those of the spectrum. As yet, I have never heard of anyone's viewing a rainbow composed of one distinct color.

Many uninformed people have declared that the paua shell, found in New Zealand, resembles opal in its colors. This shell is identical to the abalone shell, which is abundant on the California coast, but is not as large as the abalone. Jewelry fashioned from abalone shells can be seen in almost all novelty and tourist shops in California, but by no means can it be mistaken for or compared with opal.

I submitted a variety of opal specimens to Dr. Dake (mentioned above as editor of the *Mineralogist*), who has for many years made a study of opal and who has also visited the Nevada opal field at Rainbow Ridge a great number of times, studying the formations and writing numerous articles on this opal experience. Having known **Dr.** Dake for almost thirty years, I have a great respect for his professional ability and his views. The opal specimens were submitted for the purpose of obtaining his opinion regarding the various theories advanced over the years concerning these colors—colors which have thus far defied science to arrive at any satisfactory conclusion about their origin. Dr. Dake wrote, with regard to the colors in the submitted specimens, that he had nothing definite to offer on the subject of their nature or the unknown causes of their origin. Listed below are the remarks that I made to him concerning the specimens.

1. Taking your loupe and viewing this specimen, you will observe that the distinct lines are parallel, such as those found in some agate. Also note that on any orientation the colors all remain constant. Certainly there are no grounds for any optical effect.

2. Holding this specimen up to the light so as to obtain a good effect for the green color, now rotate it, and the green color will give an extinction angle at about 190° while the red color will not.

3. This specimen is of azure blue. Regardless of any orientation, the color remains constant.

4. This specimen has the parallel lines with mixed colors making a filling in between.

5. Here is a specimen which shows the precious opal as only part of the whole. This shows, if anything, a filling of the precious opal colors in the section. What caused only part of these colors to appear? Certainly no optics resulted in this.

6. This specimen is very interesting. Orient it, and you will observe that the vivid red color turns to green and vice

versa, but a small section of the red color does not change at all. Why?

7. I have circled a section on this specimen, which shows precious opal encircling the common opal. Why did this occur?

8. Notice the heavy green line of color in this specimen which is surrounded by many other colors. The heavy line is of a green color distinct from the rest.

9. This specimen is of azure blue and green only, with no red or any other colors. If any optical theory held water, the other colors would have to be present and show.

10. View this specimen with a loupe. Note how the colors all blend (blue and green only) and range from thin to heavy textures, showing, if anything, a definite filling or impregnation. Also note that the parallel lines that appear in similar specimens are in this particular case bent.

11. Note the straight lines of color in this specimen, which penetrates the matrix of common opal.

If one should ask for my opinion on which field produces the opal finest for its beauty of colors, the answer would unquestionably be: the opal from the Rainbow Ridge mine in Humboldt County, Nevada. In its breath-taking display of colors of every variety, no opal from either Mexico or Australia can match it in beauty. It is unfortunate, though, that because of its tendency to craze or to spider-web fracture after exposure to the atmosphere, it is not suitable for being fashioned into gems. Nevertheless, it still commands a very high price as a museum piece or as a cabinet specimen for the collector.

But, as Dr. Dake has learnedly pointed out, until the problem of the cause of colors in opal is solved, science will never be able to produce the gem synthetically.

3 Opal Types and Colors

ALL OPALS with a play of vivid colors can be considered precious opals. Because some opals show a predominance of red color, many term this type fire opal. In Australia, the main source of gem opal, I found this term was not used; all opals were described as precious regardless of color. It has been noted that a great many opal enthusiasts in the United States prefer the red colors more or less as the favorite. But the fine jewelry stores in Australian cities charge just as much for the vivid green and blue opals, which show no red flashes whatever. For some unknown reason I noticed that the white milk-opal variety, which usually has only the red color dominating, was not on sale in the jewelry stores of Australia. I found that this type of opal was mainly shipped overseas in its rough condition to Japan and also to the amateur lapidary trade in the United States.

Jewelry stores in Australia I considered equal to any I have observed in London, New York, or elsewhere. Their windows had grand displays of diamonds, rubies, and emeralds, as well as domestic sapphires of every shade and color and, of course, the very finest of opals. I had great respect for the ethical way in which they conducted the business; during my many trips, not overlooking any of these fine establishments, I never observed a single synthetic gem stone of any kind. They featured nothing but genuine gem stones.

Some opal of the finest quality was priced as high as $100 per karat. I especially remember a two-piece opal (doublet) unmounted, rounded slightly, and egg-shaped in its general appearance; it was approximately two inches in length, prob-

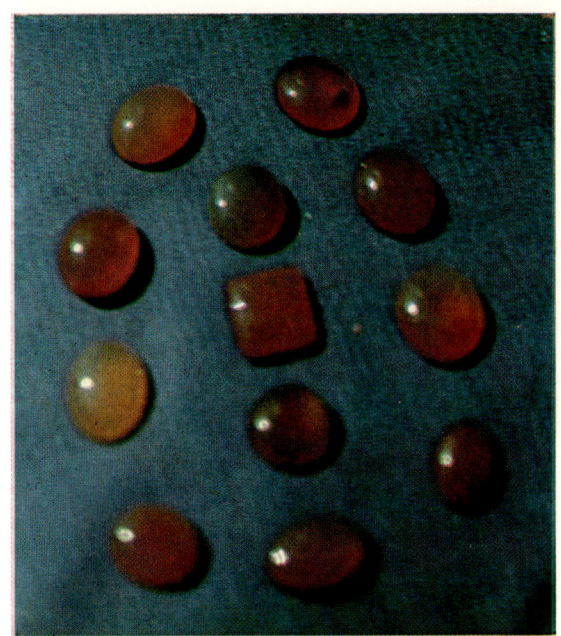

Plate 10: Mexican cherry and honey opal from the Querétaro mines.

Plate 11: Cut and polished black opal gem of $49\frac{1}{2}$ carats. From the Rainbow Ridge Mine, Nevada. Courtesy of Glen Hodson.

Plate 12: A fine display of opalized shells from South Australian fields. (Photo courtesy of W. H. Walker.)

Plate 13: Large opal specimen with mosaic inlays. From Andamooka.

Plate 14: Opals mounted and surrounded by diamonds. Top-right is a blue opal, top-left a pin-fire opal, and the other six are black opals. All are said to be from the Coober Pedy field. (Photo courtesy of W. H. Walker.)

ably slightly over an inch in width, and no more than three-eighths of an inch in thickness. It was priced in Australian pounds, which I converted into dollars and found to be $650. The stone was of very choice color and would have made an outstanding brooch or pendant. Anyone with the view that a good opal is a cheap gem stone should change that view.

A term used extensively in the United States is the word "doublet," which refers to the cementing of a very thin section of outstanding opal onto a dark background, this background usually being what is called opal potch (a dark variety of opal). The trade in Australia uses the term "two-piece opal," never "doublet." Of course both terms are correct, but perhaps the trade considers that "two-piece opal" sounds better to the customer.

Many terms relating to the colors in opals are used, and one can use his own term for the colors in his opal—e.g., pin fire, fire opal, flame opal, or Harlequin opal. The last of these shows a play of colors similar in its composition to a mosaic, the colors being in patches.

There is always a great demand for opal specimens, some of which are indeed beautiful to behold and can be viewed in most collections or museums. Lately some splendid specimens have been produced at Andamooka in South Australia. This beautiful Andamooka opal coats a quarzite matrix. (Although many miners and others term this matrix sandstone, it is actually quartzite.) If the opal coating is not fractured, the cutters in Australia will saw out the choice piece of color, regardless of how thin the coating is, and shape and boat-tail the underside, which is matrix. A fine, colorful gem is then to be had. If the specimen happens to contain fractures, then it is sold as a specimen to collectors or museums. I have observed many such specimens selling for as much as a hundred dollars each, and some for much more. A high-priced specimen would probably be a piece measuring four by three or four inches and sometimes more. The famous Lightning Ridge field does not produce such specimens as those at Andamooka, because the formation there is entirely different, and the opal is found in small individual nodules. There are, of course, a great many other localities in Australia where opal has been found. Among these is Tintinbar, in New South Wales, where opal of a type very similar to that of Rainbow Ridge was discovered. It was not suitable for gems, since it had a tendency to develop cracks after exposure to the atmosphere.

Common opal is a variety that is found extensively in many areas of the United States, as well as elsewhere. It exists especially in the igneous areas where deposits of volcanic ash intrude. In the Virgin Valley area in the state of Nevada, a great amount of this material exists, and much of it is very highly fluorescent. This fluorescent variety is usually of a light greenish type which is also translucent. There also exist in this vicinity opaque varieties which do not show any fluorescent action. These have no special value outside that of providing specimens for collectors. Much of this opal is in large veins (some eight inches thick) embedded in a huge deposit of diatomaceous earth.

A very large area of common opal exists about five miles northeast of the town of Milford in Utah. The opal here is unlike that in the Virgin Valley deposits in Nevada, for it is extremely brittle and crumbles easily. It contains some very nice colors, which are derived from iron stains permeating it. This large deposit lies on the surface, and when I visited it I could see that much of it had been mined out by some enterprising individuals who believed that it had some commercial value as ornamental or building stone. But because of its crumbly action it was worthless. These mining folks had opened up a large pit which was five feet deep and covered a hundred square feet. I inspected the entire area and found this opal deposit to cover several acres. It was comprised solely of common opal.

This deposit was in an igneous area and had been created through hydrothermal action in volcanic ash; it also contained much hyalite (clear) opal, which was observed in botryoidal form and was clear as glass. In many places where basalt occurs, this form of hyalite opal is sometimes found, usually in the form of clear botryoidal globules, coating the rock or in the vugs.

Opal in a great many cases is a replacement of fossils, wood, bone, and shells. In these cases such replacement in mineralogy is termed a pseudomorph. Many writers have mentioned that opal from Rainbow Ridge in Nevada is a replacement of wood, but not all of it is. These wood replacements are not peculiar to this location alone. I have observed pieces of wood replacement as thick as one's wrist which, when sawed, showed thousands of beautiful specks of opal of every conceivable color. I have mined out opal that had absolutely no identity whatever, being solid opal. In the case of wood-replacement specimens, the wood structure could be easily observed, for this structure was well preserved. Then again, the great mass of common opal peculiar to the area mentioned above was not a replacement of wood. Its existence as a thick vein in a diatomaceous earth deposit definitely shows that it was deposited by hydrothermal action and a definite mineralization.

Opal at White Cliffs in New South Wales, Australia, produces the very finest specimens of cockleshell and clamshell replacements, but some shells and other marine fossils from this locality are plain shells with no opal replacement. The area here dates back to the Upper Cretaceous period, a geological series which abounds in western New South Wales.

In the state of Queensland the opal is again entirely different from that found in New South Wales or South Australian fields. Here a great many small prospects have been uncovered, extending in a large area in the southwest part of the state, around Cunnamulla, Opalton, Yowah, and Quilpie. All this area is virgin land and very difficult to travel unless one has his own means of transportation; in some parts the only habitations for hundreds of miles are huge sheep or cattle ranches (called stations in Australia) which cover many thousands of acres each. The towns en route are very small, and although they do have hotel accommodations where the traveler can obtain rooms and meals, they are very primitive. Roads in all this huge area are mainly what could be termed wagon-wheel tracks; none are improved. At Quilpie, beautiful stringers of opal occur in a ferruginous hard siliceous matrix; when these stringers are closely situated, a very fine gem stone can be cut from them. Most of the material is also valuable for its specimen beauty.

At this locality, unlike all the others, it is really an outcrop, situated on the side of a creek bank. Miners obtain many fine specimens simply by breaking up the iron-colored rock, which is sometimes impregnated with colored stringers of a flashing red color. It is known as boulder opal. In another chapter, I shall more fully describe these areas and their background and history.

4 White Cliffs

WHITE CLIFFS: an interesting name, to be sure. And here it was that opal commercial history was really first made, before the other great discoveries had yet taken place. It was the forerunner of things to come. White Cliffs is 60 miles northwest of the small town of Wilcannia and 674 miles northwest of Sydney. The average rainfall is about seven to ten inches a year; the daily temperature is rarely under 100 degrees; and there is no shade.

The discovery of opal at White Cliffs had much in common with other similar discoveries. Out on the Momba sheep station, an old sheep herder, George Montgomery, was searching for water in a parched wilderness. (Water was far more valuable than opal.) There was not a living soul for miles; no habitation—just distance, saltbush, and mulga; a few elevations called hills here and there; a few small stunted trees and bushes marking a dry creek.

It was summer, and a lovely day. The old sheep man (even if he did not know it) was walking over the bottom of a prehistoric ocean. Above him was a clear cloudless blue sky and a stillness that one would have to experience to really understand. But the old man was seeking water and, he thought, with scant hope of finding it. But he might come across a waterhole in one of the ravines—maybe just enough water for a few head of sheep—for after thunderstorms at that time of year some water would lie, but not for long, since the porous sandy loam of the surface soon absorbed it.

Conserving his energy, he would climb the gentle slope of a little hill, shade his eyes from the sun, and gaze off into

1. Lightning Ridge
2. White Cliffs
3. Quilpie
4. Yowah
5. Eulo
6. Andamooka
7. Coober Pedy
8. Opalton
9. Tintinbar

Figure 1: Map of Australian Opal Fields

the distance, seeking some indication, watching the myriads of birds, for they usually led to water or a patch of green vegetation. The little hills were of a chalky nature; of course this was a capping consisting of clay that miners afterwards termed "gray billy." This gray billy was a dense silicified cap rock, and nature evidently had used it to preserve the little hills from erosion through the ages of storm and stress. Under the cap rock the eroding clay resembled white cliffs. This was where time and weather had worn away the rock, leaving crumbly heaps of softer material from under the cap. The old sheep man came upon one where those crumbled eroded clays lay. Stooping down, he picked up the curious-looking stone, a peculiar stone to him, and as clean as if it had been placed there by some former traveler, perhaps an aboriginal native. He mused a while. Was it a piece of glass? He cracked one piece with another; it splintered. Surely it must be glass. But then no one had ever been at the place, and since there was no water, the natives would never have camped there. He figured it had been there a long, long time—probably long before either white man or native.

He decided it had to be glass, but certainly not like any man-made glass he had ever seen, and the natives never made or had glass. At last he concluded that it could have resulted from some volcanic eruption (of course there is no volcanic area anywhere in the vicinity). However, he was puzzled and, of course, understandably, for this sheep man know nothing of geology or mineralogy and did not know that he was traversing an ancient inland sea bottom. And if he had known, he couldn't have cared less.

For here at one time the ocean had been, and the proof showed everywhere in opalized clams and other marine remains. These opalized clamshells later were found, absolutely intact but now entirely replaced by as beautiful an opal as one ever gazed upon. Eventually fish and other denizens of the deep were to be unearthed here, where a lonely old sheep man was trying to figure things out. Tufted grass was flourishing upon the warm earth; here all around were the sands and clays of that bygone sea, ages ago compressed into its present formation. But no water for his sheep. The irony of it all was that here at a former age had rolled a great sea. The old man picked up a stick and scratched around the chalky dirt where he had found the glasslike stones, finding at last a small seam of them, laid there by the hand of nature. He sat down and broke some. Flashes of fire—some orange, some red, and a variety of other grand colors—appeared. He gazed at all the colors of the rainbow with many more added, and he was of course amazed. At last he quit and moved on. His mission was to locate water. He stared into the great and distant loneliness, then gathered up the fragments he had broken, thinking these things might be of value, and smoothed the place all over as it had been before he had disturbed it. Then he left the scene, still seeking a sign of water in the place where once, in ages past, an ocean had rolled. Montgomery did not know what he had found, but a great many of the world's discoveries of precious things have been made in a similar manner.

For many years afterwards he told of his discovery and stated that had he known what values were lying in store at those cliffs he could have been the richest man in all Australia. For later on, the finest gems the world had ever seen were to be produced from the glasslike stones of those hills.

A few years later, in 1889, a group of kangaroo hunters were in that very same vicinity of those tufted, grassy, white hills. These hunters, camping at the exact spot of Montgomery's find, were attracted by some of the chips and also other pieces which had fallen out of place by erosion. One of the group, Will Clauston, said: "Could these be opal?" For some time past, rumors had circulated in Wilcannia, where they lived, of folks up near Cunnamulla, in the state of Queensland, finding opals.

They collected some pieces of the float and took these to the Mining Register in Wilcannia to learn whether or not they had any value. It was then that the very first opals were discovered in New South Wales. And this discovery proved to be the finest and most beautiful light translucent type of opal ever found. The irony of it all was that the Supreme Being seemed to have placed such a gorgeous gem out in a desolate, lonely, uninhabited region, as though to hide it from the exploitations of man.

Up to this time, opals had been unknown in Australia, or for that matter in most other places in the world; very few people had even heard of the gem, let alone seen it in its rough state. It was around the end of 1889 that the kangaroo hunters, Richardson, Turner, Hoaley, and Clauston, filed mining rights in the township of Wilcannia to mine opal on the Momba homestead, on which White Cliffs is located. Ted Murphy, that great and distinguished gentleman who got his start as a miner of opal and later became one of the most outstanding experts and buyers of opal in the world, joined this group.

It was at White Cliffs that Murphy sank his first shaft, down only twenty feet, and sold his first production for $140. His next sale, which was to Tully Wollaston, was for $1,000. Murphy, being at this stage very inexperienced, figured that he had cleaned out the hole. Little did he know of the values that still remained when he quit the shaft, or of the depth down to the hard pan.

A few years afterwards a chap named Ed Jones, going down a few feet deeper in Murphy's abandoned shaft, uncovered opal, which he in turn sold to Murphy for $2,500. The field at White Cliffs was five miles long and approximately two miles wide, and all more or less contained valuable opal. There were such well-known places as the Four Mile, Smith's Hill, Bunker Hill, Turley's Hill, and many others; these were all worked by what is known as a "miner's right," a government act which entitles a miner to hold and work an area of 100 square feet of ground. These and many other places adjacent to White Cliffs (which was a very large field), have even up to the date of this writing never been properly prospected. The opal at White Cliffs was not as difficult to discover and mine as that at some of the other fields that were to be found later on. So there is no question but that there still remain untold riches which will at some future time be uncovered by some lucky individuals in the vast expanse.

One great disadvantage in this area is the shortage of water, and one who has never been out in the great Australian outback cannot realize the awful silence, the loneliness of this great expanse. Australians have a name for it; they call it the Never-Never. It has often been the cause of men's going insane. There probably is no other place on earth where one feels so left alone and lonely. The author has known and experienced even the jet blackness of its night. It is always well to have a candle burning in the tent, for if one goes only a few feet away at night, and does not have that guide with which to return, one can wander off and get lost. To illustrate this blackness at night: if one went outside the tent with no light and placed one's hand in front of one's face, it would be impossible to see it. White Cliffs was a haven for the paleontologist, for a great many opalized bones, tusks, clams, and vertebrae joints were uncovered. One very outstanding series of specimens were what miners called "pineapples." These showed a definite crystal formation. Actually they were pseudomorphs after gypsum, and entirely replaced by opal. It is said that some of these were sold for as much as $500. They resembled a small pineapple about fist size, usually of a hazy bluish color.

The most outstanding fossilized opal specimen ever found was the skeleton of a plesiosaurus, an extinct sea reptile. It was all complete except for the head. It was slightly over five feet in length, and all the replacement was fine opal. This outstanding and wonderful specimen would be today a priceless museum piece; however, it was all broken up and sold for its opal, its total sales bringing $1,500 at the time. Crinoids and opalized corals were in abundance, and also a large number of belemites, which were called "pipe opal" and which at one time in ages past were the horny internal structure of cuttlefish. Mussels and sea urchins were also plentiful, all having been replaced by beautiful gem opal.

A perfect dog shark, four feet in length, was also found deep down in the clay beneath the cretaceous crust of sandstone; its head, especially the mouth, was opalized horizontally; the eye sockets were very distinct, and the body part was ringed perpendicularly with opal, the tail being flat and tapered. Flesh does not opalize, as Mr. Pittman, the Australian geologist, pointed out at the time, contending that the specimen could not possibly have been a fish. However, it was argued by others that fish had been imprisoned in the clays and that they had retained their solidity long enough to leave a mould which later had filled with opal and siliceous material.

It has been stated by the highest authorities that had the Australian government bought and preserved all these remarkable and outstanding specimens, it today would have the finest collection in the world of these grand and extinct items. As it was, a few odd pieces found their way into museums all over the world. I did observe a few now on display in the Australian National Museum in Sydney, but these are mostly of a poor or secondary nature. I can point out that Australia is not alone in this situation, for even here in California, where some of the world's finest mineral specimens were produced from the Mother Lode country and from our famous gem locations of Pala and Mesa Grande in San Diego County—here where the world's finest groups of tourmaline ever found were produced—few specimens remain. I observed years ago these grand groups mined from one mine alone, the Tourmaline King, owned at that time by my good friend, the late Mr. R. M. Wilke of Palo Alto, California. Today there is not a single specimen from that period on exhibit in any California museum.

It was not long after Ted Murphy actually mined opal that he became very proficient as a valuator. Good valuators of opal were indeed scarce, for one has to realize that in those days the modern lapidary equipment that we possess today did not exist, and each piece of opal had to be snipped at various spots to determine its color and value. Even today at Andamooka and Coober Pedy, the most active mining fields, the valuator still uses this method of determining the value. The field always had various buyers present, many of whom resided in the field, and as they made their purchases, their parcels were forwarded overseas.

During this period Tully Wollaston hired Ted Murphy to be his representative, and Murphy was given unlimited funds. He annually purchased opal amounting in value to over $250,000. In his time he paid as much as $500 for some stones and even as much as $5,000 for some outstanding pieces. This type of man is exceedingly rare today.

To give some idea of the activity that arose in this barren, off-the-beaten-track area, I may mention that White Cliffs boasted of five hotels. Of course these were of a makeshift type; however, even today country or outback hotels are still rather primitive. The town even had a race course of sorts and also several churches. Most of the water had to be hauled in from Wilcannia, sixty miles away to the south, and beer and groceries had to be packed in by camel trains. Today there is very little activity going on, outside of a few old-timers, mostly pensioners, who are of the type that never give up and hope to strike it rich once again.

5 Queensland

ALTHOUGH the discovery of opal at White Cliffs in New South Wales in 1885 was really the first in a commercial sense, the very first discoveries of opal in Australia were made about 1875 in the southwest section of Queensland, over 300 miles north of White Cliffs. In this region of Queensland is a strip of ferruginous sandstone hundreds of miles long. It traverses such places as Eulo, Yowah, Cunnamulla, and Quilpie. The fantastic escarpments of long-dead mountain ranges, these ironstone boulders lie in all directions, as if they had been tossed about by some prehistoric giant. Like other opal areas, this forbidding but fascinating country is lacking in water. No one seems to know just who he was—the wanderer in this desolation who first (probably by chance) found opal in Australia. Here in this lonely outback he was in all probability digging to obtain water, since there is always an abundance of food from kangaroos and other creatures, and water was what was necessary for his survival. Who would dream that he was in the presence of the most vividly colored gem in the world?

This wanderer who first found what is now called a Yowah nut probably thought it was some type of petrification, perhaps a nut from a prehistoric forest. When he cracked the nut open, he was stunned by the myriad of colors: fire red, green, and orange. One can imagine his feelings in that desolate, uninhabited region, gazing at the most beautiful thing nature ever created. Today the region is very much the same as it was then, outside of the fact that rich sheep stations now graze hundreds of thousands of both sheep and cattle. Some of these ranches, in fact, are as large as the state of Delaware.

It was thus that the Yowah nuts were discovered, and today the location is on the station property of the Yowah homestead, which is not marked on most Queensland maps. Almost about the same time, boulder opal was discovered at Quilpie, Quilpie being approximately 50 miles east of Yowah homestead and at the terminus of the railroad west from Brisbane. The opal from Quilpie was usually a beautiful coating on fractured portions of the ironstone rock; it also permeated it in many cases as minute veinlets all through the matrix. It resulted in gorgeous specimens, and even at the time of this writing it is still highly treasured by the gem-and-mineral collector. In some cases it also was cut and polished into gems. The Australian lapidary cut off the coating if it was sufficiently beautiful and fracture-free, and in that case it produced an outstanding gem stone.

It is said that about 1875, before these outstanding localities received any great publicity, here and there in that uninhabited bushland an occasional prospector or wanderer, blessed with that natural curiosity that urges one to examine anything which is unusual, stumbled upon the gem. Some just rode away, never understanding what they had found. Odd ones in due time came back to civilization to make inquiry as to whether what they had found had any value, and at the time were all invariably advised that it had none, and also that no market existed for it.

Then, in 1878, a miner by the name of Paddy Green found opals in the Thackaringa Hills and named the place the Aladdin Mine. Opals here were so beautiful and so plentiful that they blazed a path of glory. When Paddy named it the Aladdin, he wished for Aladdin's lamp to guide him to this mine of fiery gems. But his dreams never brought him the bounty he had found. Then also was founded the Scotchman Mine near Coonavalla, on the Euronghella homestead.

The quantity and also the quality of these magnificent gems caused people to remark that surely there must be something in them. These beautiful things of nature must be of value somewhere in the world.

In the small town of Toowoomba in the state of Queensland, which is approximately 100 miles due west of Brisbane, lived Herb Bond. Bond went off to London to try and find a market for opal, but his efforts were a complete failure. The London gem merchants absolutely refused to buy them. Their attitude was one of suspicion, and they told Bond that the stones could not possibly be opal. In all the gem markets of the European capitals, these merchants were used only to the pale milky Hungarian opal from the mines in Cyschewentza in Hungary. These mines had been worked since the end of the fourteenth century.

These new brilliant and fiery opals, blazing with all the colors of the rainbow, were unknown to these worldly experts, who suspiciously refused them. Most of them did not even know there was such a place as Australia; they smiled knowingly at any suggestion that precious opals had been unearthed in this unknown wilderness of Australia. So any early promise of acceptance for the gem was indeed very discouraging.

It was in 1889, seventeen years after opals were first found, that Tully Wollaston took his first parcel to London and began a heartbreaking struggle to gain recognition for them. Tully Wollaston came from the city of Adelaide, in the state of South Asutralia. He was a man of small stature who had a special interest in mineralogy and gems and who, after great hardships and reverses, placed Australian opal on the world market. An Adelaide lawyer named Dave Tweedie, impressed by the young Wollaston, agreed to form a partnership with him. They formed a company and obtained finances.

Wollaston then resigned from his job as a surveyor, said goodbye to his wife and small baby, and with his other partner, Herbert Buttfield, traveled northeast from Adelaide to Hergott Springs, riding horseback and camelback ever on into the mirages of South Australia's far north, then across into southwest Queensland, headed for a phantom locality named the Kyabra Hills, a place about 75 miles north of Quilpie. It was a wild-goose chase, everyone said, from which he might never return. This prophecy almost came true, for death was beckoning back of a mirage for Herb Buttfield, and it was he who perished of thirst.

It would certainly appear that Wollaston had taken a foolish risk in giving up his steady job, leaving his wife and baby of only a few weeks to whom he was greatly attached, going out into this desolate and unknown country, and seeking these opals (if they could be obtained) from an indifferent miner named Joe Bridle, who was supposed to have made a strike of rich opal somewhere in that vast area of southwest Queensland in a district only vaguely called the Kyabra Hills. At that, the rumor was three years old. Wollaston and his associates could never learn whether the rumor was even true or not, let alone whether this Joe Bridle was still in that unknown area, almost a thousand miles away in another state. A gambler would never have given any odds, for the odds against success would have been a million to one. It was a very remarkable achievement made by this South Australian, who mainly through his efforts at White Cliffs and in Queensland was to make Australian opals famous throughout the world. But destiny had already decreed that his homeland state of South Australia itself was in later years to benefit greatly from its treasure chests at Coober Pedy and

Andamooka, which at the time of this writing are producing some of the most valuable opal yet found.

Wollaston and Buttfield reached Hergott Springs, having set out by horse and camel on a 700-mile ride. In due time they crossed over the Queensland border after what would today be termed incredible hardships, including that of flies and other insects swarming everywhere in droves. (I can attest to the fact that these flies are the world's most persistent. One cannot shoo them away; one must simply and constantly swat them when they alight on one's face. Even the ants are an inch in length, and the poor horse is almost driven mad by them.)

A surprising thing was that they found tough old Joe Bridle camped at a site called Stony Creek. To Wollaston's delight, tough old Joe really did have an opal mine, and some grand opals too. He did not show these immediately, for he had that reserve and secretiveness that all true miners possess. At first he showed Wollaston only the poorer material, although how any miner in the field with opal could determine its quality I have never understood. For some time he analyzed Wollaston and Buttfield, and it was not until he felt certain that these strangers were genuine that he produced his outstanding material. And it was then that Wollaston went berserk with delight.

Now, with a lighter heart and with enlightened hope and determination, after almost 3,000 miles of grueling hardships covered by horse and camel and at time by buckboard, coach, and river boat, Wollaston returned to Adelaide, carrying with him a parcel of outstanding gems. The next problem was this: could his small syndicate gather enough funds for him to proceed to London to try and sell the gems? This they did, but before he left, he received word from the police at Windorah in Queensland that his pal Herb Buttfield had perished of thirst while he was tracking down his runaway camels in the waterless bush. Windorah is approximately 130 miles north west of Quilpie, where Buttfield had been left for future contacts.

At last in London, bitter disappointment awaited. Wollaston found, exactly as Bond had found, that the large gem merchants of Hatton Garden first viewed the beautiful gems with curiosity and then glanced at the seller with suspicion. They shook their dubious heads. No, they distinctly declared. There was no market in London for such opals. Furthermore, they did not believe they were genuine opals, having had experience with the milky, pale Hungarian variety only. Some were openly suspicious and also wondered how it was possible for such ignorant "primitives" as the wild Australian bushmen to have made these beautifully colored fakes.

Today it is almost unbelievable that the most beautiful gem the world has ever known should have been rejected as a fake and a fraud by the acknowledged experts of the world's gem markets, but it is true. After three months of great embarrassment and discouragement, Wollaston at last interested Hasluck Brothers of Hatton Garden, who were ready to give the new opals a chance. They examined them with every known test of their trade. They also decided to cut and polish some and, with these, try the United States market at Maiden Lane in New York. It was still a gamble and a small market at first—just a trickle. Later it was to grow into a flood that firmed, once they had started and had really introduced them to the world at large. After this initial introduction, Wollaston returned to Australia, and since the field at White Cliffs had been discovered and was producing, had such famous opal men as Ted Murphy and others on his staff buying opal to send overseas to fill orders for the gem that now had been accepted all over the world, not only by Hatton Garden but Maiden Lane, Paris, and Berlin as well.

Today this trade is still with us. Opal has been found over

a very large area in Queensland. Those who have pioneering stamina still uncover some; no doubt in the years ahead more will be heard of rich strikes. For it is impossible to imagine that such a vast area has been entirely prospected or all its fields worked out. If one takes a map of the state of Queensland and looks up the various places where opal has been found, he will arrive at the enormous area these places cover. Quilpie, Opalton, Cunnamulla, Kyabra Hills, and Eulo are just a few of the places where the gem has been obtained. Many of these places are widely separated, and all are in the southwest portion of the large state. In fact, the largest opal of gem quality ever found was unearthed on the Opalton field in 1898. This was a replacement of a tree limb and was ten feet long by one foot in diameter. Green miners of the period, having absolutely no knowledge of opal or its value, smashed it up. Even as a museum piece this specimen would be worth millions today; in fact, it would be priceless.

6 The Eulo Queen

IT WAS somewhat of a coincidence that two women separated by thousands of miles were to play a great part in the early days of opal-mining history, one at Rainbow Ridge in Nevada and the other at Eulo in the southwestern part of Queensland, Australia. These remarkable ladies were Mrs. F. H. Lockheed, whom we shall meet in a later chapter, and the lady known as the Eulo Queen, who makes her appearance here.

No one seems to know how the lady who was known as the Eulo Queen arrived at such an outlandish place as Eulo, which is in Queensland, 500 miles due west of Brisbane. If one views a map of that state, he will note that it appears to be fairly well populated, for the map shows a great many names. But these are in the main not towns at all but mostly homesteads: large sheep or cattle stations. When one gets away from the coastal areas and goes west, any place with a population of a few hundred is quite a large town. Eulo was only a small hamlet; its population was never more than a hundred people, even in the days of opal mining in the vicinity (around 1900). At this period it took at least a week of travel to get from Brisbane to Eulo, and travel was mainly by horse, some parts perhaps by coach. The Queen reigned there till about 1918, on and off.

She was said to be very beautiful, with a nice figure, a flawless complexion, and light-brown hair. She dressed beautifully in the latest styles of the period and wore the most expensive jewelry, certainly looking the part of a queen. Her first business venture was the operation of a grog shanty at

Eulo on the banks of the Paroo River. At this time her real name was not known, but she went by the name of Maggie. It was said that at the age of fourteen she had married a man named McIntosh, and when this marriage was later annulled, she married a gent named Robinson, who just disappeared.

In her forties she married a laborer named Gray, who was sixteen years her junior. Gray enlisted in World War One, and what became of him afterwards is not known. At this period she was operating a small hotel, with a kind of general store attached. When Gray was part of the family, she often had him arrested for stealing from the store, and once he was sentenced to a jail term in Boggo Jail in Brisbane for it. It was said that that was the only work he ever did. But despite this, she always welcomed him back with open arms and put on a big celebration. She had a phobia about people stealing from her, and she wore a belt with many keys dangling from it. In 1908 the Queen gave her age as forty-five, and it is said she looked no more. She then went by the name of Isabella Gray. It is known that she had a valuable opal collection, probably the finest in the world at that period. What became of it in later years, no one ever knew.

The Queen gave elaborate parties for only the rich graziers and opal miners from the surrounding mining areas, places such as Yowah, Southern Cross, Duck Creek, Humeburn, Cunnamulla, and Opalton. It was from these gentlemen that she obtained her hoard of opals. Since opal was being mined down south at White Cliffs in New South Wales, many of the miners from there drifted north to the strikes in Queensland. It was natural to assume that these men brought some opal with them, which added to the Queen's lot. Many of these were soldiers of fortune, like those always to be found whenever strikes of gems or minerals are discovered. A recent illustration of this was seen here in the United States with the rush to the uranium strikes in Utah and Colorado. The Queen never paid any attention to the local cowhands or sheep herders. She never gave them a second look; if they were not in the money or in opal, they wasted their time.

It was said that the Eulo Queen's greatest delight was the exploitation of unfortunates who came into her employ. She would obtain domestics from agencies in Brisbane on the condition that fare would be paid if they stayed six months. But shortly before the six months expired, she would pick a quarrel with them and turn them adrift without home or money.

Later on in life she changed, became more benevolent, and supplied bread and goods to many deserving folks in the neighborhood; and whenever a swagman (tramp) made camp on the river bank below her store, she would walk down with fresh bread and groceries for him. In later years she was living alone in the old Commercial Hotel at Eulo. She was still a good-looking woman, and I found a great many of the old-timers today around Eulo and Cunnamulla who knew the Queen the whole time she was the boss and reigned at Eulo. No one now seems to know just what became of her in her old age.

An old-timer I met by the name of Sam Brodie says that when he last visited Eulo to look up the Queen in 1922, he was informed that she had been taken to a state home or institution in Brisbane, after she had tried to kill herself in a fit of depression. Doubtless she died there some time afterwards. But what became of the opals everyone knew she once owned, no one ever discovered.

7 Lightning Ridge

VERY FEW people know how this great opal field obtained its name. Probably most persons imagine that it derives the name from the beautiful colors of the gem unearthed there. This is not the case. As it happens, the name is derived from an incident related to sheep. There are very large sheep stations in the area which cover thousands of acres, but no homesteads can be seen in the vicinity. At one time before opal was discovered there, a sheep man with a small flock (as sheep flocks go) of about 300 sheep that he was driving to a grazing area got caught in a violent thunderstorm of the sort that occur rather commonly during the hot summer months. A bolt of lightning struck the flock, which was tightly packed, and almost all of it was wiped out, since wool, when wet, is a strong conductor. The early sheep men thereafter named this small ridge after the disaster.

Lightning Ridge later proved to be a very fitting appellation for the site of the most glorious gem stone ever produced in the world. The Ridge is really only a small elevated rise, at its highest point not more than about 35 feet above the surrounding flat terrain. Even so, one standing on the crest of it can peer off into space, reaching even to eternity.

A number of articles from time to time have described the area as desert. This is absolutely wrong. When I was there it was gloriously green with luxuriant grass growing everywhere, for good rains had occurred. Small stunted tree growths of eucalyptus—none of enough size to warrant commercial use—served for firewood and shade. The surface soil is red and reminds one of the soil in the American state of Georgia. The road through the small center of habitation is as red as the cliffs of the Grand Canyon. Thousands of white clay hillocks of the dumps from the shafts are to be seen for miles; these resemble giant ant hills.

The Lightning Ridge field was really first discovered by a homestead owner who sank a well to obtain water. In the heyday of great mining activity, it boasted a population of eight to ten thousand souls. These were mainly miners or other hardy souls, most of whom in those days resided in tents. At that period the railroad did not end at Walgett, 50 miles to the south, as it does now. The only way to get to the field in those early days was either on horseback or on foot. Opal had been discovered previous to Lightning Ridge both at White Cliffs, near Wilcannia, and up in Queensland at the Kyabra Hills, Quilpie, Eulo, and some other spots. When one studies the map he will observe that several thousand square miles separate these places, and since the entire area at one time was a huge inland sea, the geology of this area from White Cliffs to the fields in southern Queensland and thence to Lightning Ridge, and now on to Andamooka and Coober Pedy over in South Australia, is the same throughout. Thus it certainly stands to reason that some day another squatter or homesteader will sink a shaft for water and uncover another great field.

Opal mining at Lightning Ridge was always a hit-or-miss proposition. Some of the early-day miners sank their very first shaft and struck opal when the stratum was reached; many others sank shaft after shaft down to the stratum and finally left in disgust without ever striking any opal. It was always a great gamble, like gold or the other precious items, which the Supreme Being reveals only to some, producing great disappointment for the many.

It was said that several teams (which were mainly com-

Plate 15: Miner's shanty at Lightning Ridge. It is typical of the conditions in the area.

Plate 16: Section of the main street of the town of Lightning Ridge. The town is too busy mining opals to care for civic improvements.

Plate 17: Panoramic view of the opal dumps at the Lightning Ridge field. The opal dirt is mined and dumped around the entrance of the vertical shafts, eventually creating mounds of considerable size. This is only a small section of the countless shafts in the area.

Plate 18: A typical residence at Lightning Ridge. Note the water tank for conserving the drainage off the roof.

Plate 19: Main Street, Walgett, New South Wales. The balconied building in the center is the hotel. Walgett is a typical Australian town.

Plate 20: The train to Walgett. On this train each station is a "beer stop"—the train stops long enough for the passengers to quench their thirst.

Plate 21: The truck service from Walgett to Lightning Ridge.

posed of two men, one on top to work the windlass and the other below doing the digging) sank as many as 200 shafts and never unearthed a single opal. Yet another team only a few feet away was mining out opal valued at thousands of pounds. The one method that governs all mining is extremely hard work. All used pick and shovel and still do to this very day. Many have asked why modern methods have not been used. Some of the world's most accomplished mining men and engineers have visited the field, and if there were any other practicable method outside of pick and shovel it would have been instituted years ago.

The shafts are separated in some cases by only a few feet, and although hundreds are on the ridge itself, there are hundreds on the flat and all the way out to the Three Mile and on to the Nine Mile and then on to what is known as the Grawon. The main reason no other method is possible is that the opal dirt or stratum is never at a constant level. The depths to this stratum vary anywhere from 15 to 40 feet. A fine gravel and dirt exists for a few feet, then a sandstone formation is gone through, then a very flinty and hard quartzite is encountered. How these miners go through this material with a pick is really beyond the imagination, but they do. When the pick hits this material, chips fly off and hit the wielder in the shins; so miners never mention it by its true name but rather refer to it as "shin-cracker," an appropriate term.

At last the pick hits the grayish hard-packed clay. This is what miners call the opal dirt, really a clay. It is usually only about three feet in thickness. No opal is found deeper; hardpan exists below. Only in this clay exist what the miners call nobbies, opal in small round or almond-shaped pieces. All of the clay stratum is hoisted to the surface by a crude windlass made from a log with a crank inserted in its end. Today the miners use a wire screen, and this clay is sifted

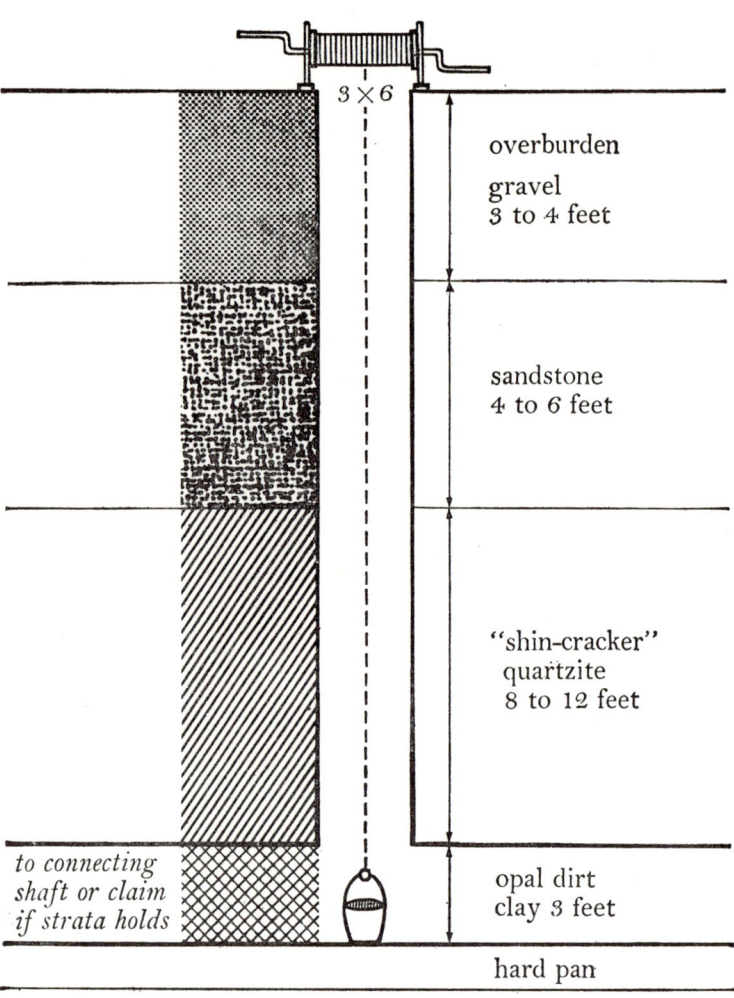

Figure 2: Typical Shaft Structure at Lightning Ridge

through it, so as not to overlook a gem which, being covered in clay, would be otherwise hard to detect. The shafts are always dug narrow, approximately two and a half feet in width, and only long enough for the miner to wield his pick.

It is interesting to observe descending miners in the shaft. They straddle the shaft, first one foot, then the other, against the wall, and they ascend the same way. One may ask why these miners use the pick to go through the hard quartzite instead of using powder or dynamite. Again this is not possible in such a narrow shaft and formation, for its use would cave in the workings.

In the days of great activity the field attracted all types of characters; some of the smartest crooks in existence were soon to arrive, and, as is usually the case, the hard-working and trustful miner was no match for these gentlemen with their marked cards and many other methods used to fleece them of the money which they made from the sale of their opal to the buyers who came from all over the world.

Not only the gambling gentry arrived but also gangs of what we in the United States know as "highgraders" came. The Australian term for these gents is "ratters." When a certain miner and his pal bottomed on opal and struck fine gems, it was only natural that in the evening around the campfire they showed the beautiful glowing gems by candle-light to the other men in camp, who would always be pleased that someone had made a strike. In the crowd looking on would be some of these ratters, who would of course overhear whose shaft had made the strike. When the miners next morning in high spirits went down the shaft, they found the ratters had cleaned the place out entirely. It became very dangerous for any team to show or boast openly of their strike or good luck, if they had bottomed on opal. Things at one time became so bad that hundreds of miners formed a vigilante committee to try and eliminate these ratters and protect the miners. But the ratters had such a good espionage system that few were ever brought to justice.

A number of outstanding buyers camped on the field, among them representatives of some of the world's largest jewel houses in London, Paris, Berlin, and Sydney. They included E. F. (Ted) Murphy, the buyer for T. C. Wollaston, and Ernie Sherman, who assembled some magnificent gems which he took to London and also to the Great Delhi Durbar in India. Sherman also made many trips to the United States. My good friend Francis S. Sperisen, a famous San Francisco lapidary, bought many of Ernie Sherman's gems. Today Sherman's son, E. Gregory Sherman, carries on in his father's footsteps in Sydney and is the largest dealer and buyer in the presently active fields at Andamooka and Coober Pedy in South Australia. He goes to these fields each month and purchases as much as $70,000 worth of opals on each trip. Another famous buyer at Lightning Ridge was Max Berlini, who was also noted for his gambling. Time after time he would go broke, but somehow he always made a strong comeback, and it would not be long before he was again paying thousands in pounds sterling for all and sundry gems that were offered. He had also previously been one of the large buyers at the White Cliffs field.

At one time a miner sold Berlini a parcel of opal for 1,800 pounds. This was during the period when one pound was worth $4.80 in exchange. Berlini at the time did not have the cash, so he sent the parcel to Sydney and waited for the returns. One day, in the meantime, a two-up gambling game started. The miner who owned the parcel got the toss and said to Berlini: "You owe me 1,800 pounds for that parcel of opal. I'll toss you double or nothing." Berlini said: "It's a deal." They tossed for the 3,600 pounds, and Berlini won the toss.

Every miner liked Berlini; he always played for big money, and when he had it, he paid top prices for big parcels, and when he went down, he always had a smile. Everyone always knew he would be on top again, and he always was. The only thing that ever got Berlini down and out was his death. He is buried at Lightning Ridge. He lived among the opals he loved. He now sleeps among them. Visitors to the ridge can ask for and be shown his grave.

Another famous buyer, who was also a miner, was Percy Marks, who made a fortune with the opal he bought and mined. Today visitors to Sydney should view one of the finest jewelry stores in existence, which his descendants operate in the Hotel Australia block on Castlereagh Street. Visitors to Sydney can also view his grand exhibit, which is on display at the Technical Museum. This collection of opals from the early days of Lightning Ridge and White Cliffs is very probably the finest extant in the world today.

Another famous buyer at the time was Bennie Solomons. He too paid a king's ransom for the gems from the Tingha. He traveled from the field to Sydney and back, buying and selling as fast as it was possible to do so. In those days travel and accommodations were very primitive indeed. Sydney, being approximately 420 miles away, probably took at least ten days to make. Solomons had come from White Cliffs, where he was hawking trinkets for an existence. Of course there were also a great many other buyers who came from the large world capitals and whose names are either lost or forgotten.

Hundreds of exciting experiences were related by both the lucky as well as the unlucky ones. Right on the crest of the Ridge two elderly gents whose names no one ever knew sank their first shaft and were rewarded with beginner's luck. They bottomed on opal. Their claim proved to be extraordinarily rich in opal. Fabulous stones came out of it

It was stated that for every 100 pounds paid by the buyers for this opal, they made 1,000 pounds' profit. These two old gents knew little of opal or opal mining. When, by sheer luck, they bottomed on rich opal, they sold the gems as fast as they mined them out and held the view that anyone foolish enough to pass out good money for such worthless material was crazy or worse. Since they always kept to themselves and had no confidants, and neither wished nor sought advice, they knew very little about what went on at the field. They were quite satisfied to sell their opal from day to day to the buyers who visited their camp. After they quit, it was thought that they had taken out all the opal dirt and that the claim was completely worked out, for they had quietly packed up and left the field. Here, perhaps, was a chance that something could have been overlooked, for opal mining was a very exacting operation and still is. The old gents could have overlooked something, and sure enough they had.

A young chap named Hugie Hughes, who had been a coal miner back in Wales before coming to Australia and who had been on the field over a year and was just getting by with spotty luck, lowered himself by the rope from the windlass above and, wall-bracing, lit a candle and looked around. The feeble light showed that the two miners had left a large pillar of the opal dirt in the center, obviously for safety purposes, in order to support the roof. The roof, however, was solid quartzite, and there was not the least danger of pressure collapsing it. Then again, the opal dirt of which the pillar consisted was clay. It was useless to support any pressure from above.

Opal was there, and a huge cavern as far as the light from the candle could be observed, and they had left piles of mullock (refuse). They had chambered far out from the shaft in an ever-widening circle; the smooth flat roof was a huge expanse of quartzite, thousands of tons of solid rock overhead, supposedly being supported by one large pillar. That solid body supported itself. Lightning Ridge was wonderful standing ground, and never a stick of timber was needed. It was readily understandable that miners not conversant with good holding formations like this should leave a massive solid block of rich opal dirt to support that vast roof. They indeed probably felt glad when they had mined out the last of their opal and scampered up the shaft to safety.

The young miner chipped away at the pillar. This opal dirt was hard packed and probably was beginning to silicify. Most opal dirt, being clay, is soft. Within ten minutes the pick hit an opal, and there under the light of the candle glowed the color of orange, green, and red fire. "The thrill and excitement of striking opal is an experience one will remember as long as he lives," Hughes said afterwards. Day after day he chipped into that pillar, only driving slowly at the rate of about a foot a day, and on opal all the time.

An opal mine has a silence all its own; of course all mines have their respective silences, but the dull silence and loneliness of an opal mine is for some unknown reason different from the rest, perhaps because it is a one-man operation down below. How strange to realize that millions of years ago waves of an ocean washed where now is the silence of an underground opal mine! Hughes worked out the large support pillar and from it realized 1,500 pounds sterling or approximately $4,200.

In the heyday of the field, there were many teams that struck it rich. There was, for instance, the pair of Jack Scott and Harry McCullum, who bottomed on a patch of opal which sold for 13,000 pounds. They obtained 100 pounds merely for the chips which were broken off the first stone (which, by the way, was shattered by the pick). McCullum owned the claim, and he had to do considerable enticing to get Scott to join him as his partner. His former partner, Bill

Henley, had given up in disgust and gone off to shear sheep at one of the large sheep stations. Henley returned after they had sunk the shaft and bottomed on the fortune. Scott called him aside and opened his can, inside of which was the glorious flash of a dozen rainbows. Every stone in that can brought over 100 pounds. There were eleven stones, and they sold for a total of 1,200 pounds. It is said that today each one of those stones would sell for 1,000 pounds.

A very notable claim was known as the Tingha. This was owned by Matty Sullivan and Paddy Kelly, two good Irishmen. They bottomed on untold riches; parcel after parcel was brought up and faced (faced means having one side ground off to show the quality and beauty). Thousands of pounds' worth were extracted, and the gems among them were of breath-taking beauty. Murphy bought almost the entire production, paying out thousands of pounds for it.

The jewel buyers of Sydney, shrewd though they were, saw the very first black opals in the world, rejected them out of hand as being worthless, and thereby lost themselves a fortune. These black opals were found at Lightning Ridge, which is situated in rather lonely country 50 miles to the north of Walgett and a little way south from the Queensland border. It is still the only place in the world where black opals of commercial quality are found.

The story of Lightning Ridge is one of faith, courage, struggle, and luck in the face of almost contemptuous disbelief and of bitter feuds at the time with reigning squatters. Although the events were accompanied by less bloodshed and notoriety, Lightning Ridge has seen as much high adventure in the Australian manner as was ever seen in the Ned Kelly bushranger country of the states of Victoria or New South Wales.

Over sixty years ago, White Cliffs, then still pouring out a wealth of opals, had its quota of miners who struck no luck, and many of them rolled their blankets and went in search of new fields or simply drifted into other jobs if mining was not deep in their blood. One of these born miners who left White Cliffs when he heard the first rumor of opal at Lightning Ridge was Charlie Nettleton.

Nettleton was the tall, lean, hard, knockabout type of bushman commonly seen in those days. He demonstrated his toughness and tenacity by walking the 400 miles from White Cliffs to Walgett during the extremely hot summer of 1901. Arriving there, he was told that gold had been found up near the Queensland border, so he walked on north only to find that the gold was mica. While he was in the border country, turning over in his mind his next action, he was advised that some boys had picked up some strange-looking black stones that flashed and gave out a whole spectrum of colors. He managed to obtain some samples and recognized them as opal. But they were of a variety he had never before seen. They were not like the opals from White Cliffs or like the beautiful opals he had seen from southwestern Queensland. They fascinated Nettleton. And well they should have, for they seemed alive, and not only did they have all the splendid colors that opal alone can produce, but they also had a velvet appearance that was somehow completely new to him.

At this time Nettleton was flat broke and unable to go in search of locations or mine for the new stones he had been shown. Then he was grubstaked by Joe Beckett, a saloonkeeper of the Wetallbar Inn, located about 10 miles from Lightning Ridge on the Walgett-to-Angledool road. Thus backed, Nettleton set about the sinking of his first shaft at Lightning Ridge on October 15, 1902. The site was close to the spot on which the government water tank for miners now stands. Nettleton obtained opal from his shaft but nothing of real value. It was the only shaft sunk there, and the remains of it, there to this day, are like a sort of inverted monument amid thousands of acres of unworked ground.

Nettleton's real lead came early in 1903 when the wife of a boundary rider showed him some outstanding black stones that the family had found while they were picnicking six miles over the ridge to the east, and where they had sunk a well for water. This proved to be a real strike and was later to become known as the Nobby's. Yet, although he did not know it, Nettleton's troubles were only beginning. Four local squatters each put up $125 (twenty-five pounds) and formed a small prospecting company, from which capital Nettleton was paid 25 shillings a week ($5.25) along with his keep. He set to work with a partner named Charlie Troy, and they soon had some parcels of very high-grade opal.

Nettleton, still fascinated by the living, velvet beauty of the gems, packed a parcel and sent it to a dealer in Sydney. The dealer wrote back that the black "nobbies" (the name given to black opals before cutting) were a near-worthless matrix (coating in which gems are often enclosed) and offered him $5 (about one pound) for the lot. Nettleton refused the offer and had his parcel returned. He sent it to other dealers, who all expressed the same opinion as the first one. So ended the opal company on Lightning Ridge.

In spite of Nettleton's failure, men were beginning to drift onto the field, and new shafts were going down in the hope of finding opals of the White Cliffs variety. Then trouble began with the squatters (homesteaders). One sheep station on which shafts were being sunk and opals found objected to the presence of the miners. They could not stop them from sinking their shafts because they held miners' rights which, in those days (as today to a lesser degree), conferred powerful privileges.

The squatters thought they saw a legal way of driving away the miners by impounding their horses, claiming that they were grazing illegally. They charged 2/6 (two shillings and sixpence or about 60 cents) for the release of every animal. That was a lot of money in those days, especially to a struggling, hard-working miner, but it was not enough to break the spirit or determination of these hardy souls who had ventured to Lightning Ridge.

So the manager of one sheep station resorted to an even more drastic method. On his station lay the only available water supply within a considerable distance, and he fenced it in, arguing that though the law allowed miners to sink shafts, it did not force him to supply them with water. A number of small drains were dug from the fenced dams so that they sloped down and beyond the fences. The station manager warned the miners that the water had been poisoned to kill rabbits. The miners didn't believe him, but none were willing to gamble. They would not even allow their horses to drink it. Instead, they traveled long distances and brought water in on pack horses—a meagre enough supply, but enough to allow them to hold out.

By this time the Simm's Hill deposits had been discovered (at Lightning Ridge) and, much to the miners' relief, it was plainly seam opal (on the white side in appearance), which they could sell. It was the Simm's Hill find that caused the first big rush to the Ridge, which took place in 1903. It also brought tougher resistance from the squatters, but the Department of Mines stepped in on the side of the miners. The squatters were prohibited from impounding the miners' horses and were also forced to give the miners access to the dams until such time as the government itself could arrange a supply.

At the beginning, the Department of Mines surveyed off 1,200 acres and declared it a mining field "within the act." This area since has been increased steadily, and today the Lightning Ridge mining field covers 50,000 acres, of which less than $2\frac{1}{2}$ percent has been worked. After the Simm's Hill find, Nettleton, disheartened by the rejection of his black opals, teamed up with Bob Bishop, a new arrival at the field, and Bishop's seventeen-year-old son. Together they went to the opal field of southwestern Queensland, but they remained there only a short while before returning to Lightning Ridge.

Nettleton was now so determined to sell his black opals that he rolled his blankets (in which he included a parcel of the gems) and set off on foot for White Cliffs. He walked the first 120 miles to Brewarrina, then worked his way from station to station until he reached Bourke. From Bourke he caught a paddle side-wheeler carrying wool down the Darling River to Wilcannia, then walked the 50 miles from Wilcannia to White Cliffs. The total distance was 400 miles—about the same as his historic walk from White Cliffs to Walgett.

At White Cliffs that great opal man and buyer Ted Murphy (author of the book *They Struck Opal*) was at the time buying for the greatest opal dealer of all time, T. C. (Tully) Wollaston. Murphy instantly recognized them as true opals and, like Nettleton, marveled at the velvet-black splendor. Murphy sent the parcel along to Wollaston, who replied instantly: "Send us all you can get." Wollaston had such faith in black opals that he immediately sent Murphy from White Cliffs to Lightning Ridge to start buying them up.

Wollaston himself had problems in getting the new black gems accepted on the trade market, but he succeeded after spending much time and money. Nettleton returned to Lightning Ridge and did well, and after some time the government paid him a paltry 250 pounds, or about $1,250, for the part he had played in giving the black opal to the world. As with so many romantic figures of the times, luck and fortune did not stay with Nettleton, and he died in Sydney, flat broke, in 1948.

The Lightning Ridge he founded and made world-famous was to have many colorful characters, some of whom are still there today living in shanties that they made upwards of half a century ago. Old Fred Bodel is one such old-timer. Fred was working as a station (sheep) hand in the vicinity of Lightning Ridge before opal was found there. He was the man responsible for the finding in 1929 of the beautiful opal known as the Pandora Star, which, unlike most of the opals at Lightning Ridge, was white.

This is the way it happened. Bodel tossed a coin with a friend, Jack Nicols: heads, Nicols was to start a new shaft; tails, he was to clean out an old one. The coin fell heads, and Nicols walked over to the spot where the coin had fallen and marked out a shaft around it. The day chanced to be a Friday, and Nicols, like many old-timers, was a superstitious man and regarded it as bad luck to begin sinking a shaft on a Friday. So he went home to camp, and spent the evening trying hard to get Bodel to come into partnership with him on the new shaft. Bodel refused; he preferred to work on the old shaft. A few days later and only 15 feet down, Nicols found the Pandora Star. Bodel's own description of it was: "big as a man's forearm, and shaped much the same." In fact, Bodel thought it had formed around a fossilized bone. Nicols received 220 pounds for the Pandora Star, or about $1,200. Today it is in the United States and is said to be valued at 65,000 pounds or about $146,000.

Although Bodel missed out on the Pandora Star, he struck it rich in 1907, when he and a partner struck one of the richest patches of opal ever found at Lightning Ridge. It is today known as the New Chum Diggings, and Bodel and his partner had bought it only a few days earlier for 30 shillings or about $7.50 from a man named Ned Plunk, who had no luck and had quit it. Just how lucky can one get? Bodel and his pal cut through the opal dirt until they came upon a fault (a break in the formation) resulting from earth movement, and it was in this fault that they found an immense deposit of opal. In the picturesque words of Bodel, "We dug out opal like potatoes. I've never before or since seen nobbies so thick." Murphy bought the whole of the great find. He would come along each evening and buy the day's production, which would be spread out in a grocery box. In those days the demand was for first-class gems with red fire. There was little or no sale for the green or blue types, which today bring not less than $40 to $50 a carat. The area from which Bodel and his partner got all their opal was about 20 feet long and 8 feet wide, and from it they took opal for which they received 1,210 pounds or $6,000, at prices ranging from one shilling to two shillings sixpence (25 to 50 cents) a carat. Today, with the enormous interest in and demand for opal, the gems they won would be worth from 20 to 100 pounds per carat or from $45 to $225 at the present rate of exchange—a great deal more than a million pounds.

Lightning Ridge has produced many noteworthy gems. One of these is the Light of the World, a beautiful dish-shaped black opal with blood-red fire moving throughout the gem. Little is known of its early history or of who mined it. It is now in the United States and is said to be valued at $225,000. Then there is the Red Emperor, also known as the Pride of Australia, which was found 70 feet down on the Three Mile workings at Lightning Ridge. Like many great opals, it was sold for a song, and today, after changing hands many times, it is worth a king's ransom. (Incidentally, one of the most striking features out at the Three Mile at Lightning Ridge, even today, is the great area of unworked ground around it.) There is also the Flame Queen, mined by

Jack Phillips and his two partners at the Bald Hill workings. Today this opal is said to be worth 15,000 pounds ($33,750), but Phillips and his partners had to accept 75 pounds ($375) for it. Why? Because they were so poor that they had been living on hotcakes and syrup for three weeks.

The Three Mile, which is the largest workings at the Ridge, was first discovered in 1908, but the big rush did not take place until the following year, when as many as 1,400 miners camped on what is now known as Nettleton's Flat. Today, there is very little left of the flourishing township of a half century ago. A few shanties still remain and traces of a sly-grog shop which for some unknown reason seems strange in a mining community and which would serve liquor only by daylight. Nothing remains of the other stores, or the boardinghouse that catered to 35 guests at one pound a week each, or the school, or the dance hall named after Charlie Nettleton.

But it is heartening to know that world demand for the black opal is again great, for this means that Lightning Ridge has a future. Although much of the past has gone, and the old shanties are fast disappearing, a new town is growing up, and the present population is about 180. For example, the town now has a council for the first time, and it is proposed to spend 65,000 pounds ($146,250) this year on public improvements. Arrangements are now being made for water to be laid on, and then the old days of tanks will be gone; a new police station and courthouse are now almost completed. The hospital and the school are up to date, and there are two stores, a butcher, a baker, a garage, a post office, and, of course a pub, in which I already have been a guest.

Holidaymakers who care to visit Lightning Ridge may themselves strike it lucky, for there is still opal lying around in the dumps, which even the veriest townsman may find.

Recently four lads from the town of Newcastle near Sydney holidayed at the Ridge. They camped out at the Three Mile, and, after spending a day or two sight-seeing, decided to work through some of the old dumps. They uncovered a very fine 14-carat green opal which they sold for 150 pounds ($337.50).

We should all pay homage to the early-day prospectors, such as Charlie Nettleton and Fred Bodel at Lightning Ridge. They had much in common with other prospectors the world over. It is a remarkable and significant fact that the great majority of these men were gifted with but little education. They knew absolutely nothing of the science of geology or mineralogy; even so, it was these men all over the world who mainly uncovered the riches the earth contained. I have visited many fields and have even played a part in many famous mineral strikes, but I have known only one man educated in the science of geology who ever made an outstanding discovery. The lone individual was a Canadian mining engineer who discovered a rich diamond field in Central Africa. I remember a student's asking a professor of geology why, if he understood the earth's formations, he didn't go forth and unearth some riches. The science of geology and mineralogy studied in the classroom sounds quite simple; applying it in the field is an entirely different matter indeed.

Every great discovery and rich strike, such as that of gold back in 1849 in California; the great gold discoveries at Ballarat and Bendigo in Australia; those on the Rand in South Africa; the famous strike in the Yukon territory (the Klondyke) at Dawson city, in which I played a part, and such other places as Goldfield, Tonopah, Rawhide, Candelaria, and Rhyolite in Nevada; the great copper-deposit finds in Montana and Arizona at Butte, Bisbee, and Tombstone; the silver finds in the Calico Mountains in San Bernardino

County in California and the Comstock Lode in Nevada, which provided hundreds of millions of dollars in the early days of San Francisco's history; the gold at Yellow Knife in northern Ontario; the pitchblende at Great Bear Lake in northern Canada; our own uranium deposits in recent years in Utah and Colorado; and, of course, many others—every last one of these discoveries was made by hardy and mainly unschooled prospectors such as Charlie Nettleton and Fred Bodel.

The mining engineer and the geologist came in later with the production and development. But almost all the original discoveries were made through the efforts of the usually bewhiskered prospector, who very rarely obtained more than a pittance for the discovery.

8 Andamooka

AT THE present time, this is the most productive field; therefore I intend to elaborate very fully on the geology and other factors of the field and its operations. The grade of opal mined is in the main of very fine quality, although the field produces a great deal of the white or milk opal variety, which does not command a high price in the gem trade. At the same time opal is mined that is of as high a grade as at any of the other fields.

The Andamooka field is situated about 140 miles north of Port Augusta, on the west side of Lake Torrens, and about 8 miles distant from the northwestern corner of the lake. The usual route to the field is by the east-west train to Pimba, 113 miles from Port Augusta, then by mail truck for about 65 miles, as far as Andamooka Homestead. The field is about 30 miles farther north, and this last journey must be covered by a prearranged method of transportation or with the driver of the local mail and supply truck, which runs once a week between the field and the homestead. The opal field is in the northern part of the Andamooka Homestead and between Pimba Ridge and Teatree Creek, which runs eastward to Lake Torrens and is about $4\frac{1}{2}$ miles north of Pimba Ridge. A tributary of Teatree Creek, namely Opal Creek, has its headwaters on the northern side of Pimba Ridge and passes through the center of the opal field, flowing in a northeasterly direction for a distance of about 5 miles from its source.

The oldest rocks in the locality are of unknown age (Paleozoic or even older) and consist of thin-bedded purple and green slates or shales which have been proved through boring to be at least 260 feet in thickness. Good exposures of these slates occur on the northern bank of Teatree Creek at Red Cliffs waterhole, where a thickness of 45 feet is plainly visible, and on the banks of Trig Creek (a tributary of Teatree Creek) at the foot of Trig Bluff, and in the bed of Opal Creek east of One Tree Hill, as well as at other localities on Andamooka Homestead. At Red Cliffs, the slates are horizontally bedded, but at Trig waterhole the strike of the slates is 28° W. of N. (magnetic), and the dip is to the northeast at an angle of 8°. Some of the slates are finely laminated and show ripple marks, indicative of shallow-water conditions at the time of their deposition.

Upon these slates is a massive bed of purplish and brown quartzite which is estimated to be at least 250 feet in thickness. In part, the quartzites are much decomposed to form a sandstone. The basal beds of quartzite were deposited in thin layers and in shallow water, as evidenced by the extensive current-bedding and ripple marks present in all of the outcrops throughout the district. On passing up the series, the quartzite becomes more massive. These quartzites form a high tableland, extending from the western shores of Lake Torrens (about one mile south of Teatree Creek) westward for at least 14 miles and southward for at least 12 miles. An east-west fault scarp marks the northern edge of the quartzite tableland, about one mile north of the Pimba Ridge. Thin current-bedded purplish decomposing quartzite and grit are exposed in the bed of Opal Creek, about $1\frac{1}{2}$ miles north of the scarp. A wedge of thin current-bedded quartzite is exposed in the northern bank, at the junction of Opal Creek with Teatree Creek, where the bed attains a thickness of only 15 feet. The quartzites are lying conformably upon thin-bedded purplish slates, with dolomite limestones above the quartzite. The strike of the rocks at this

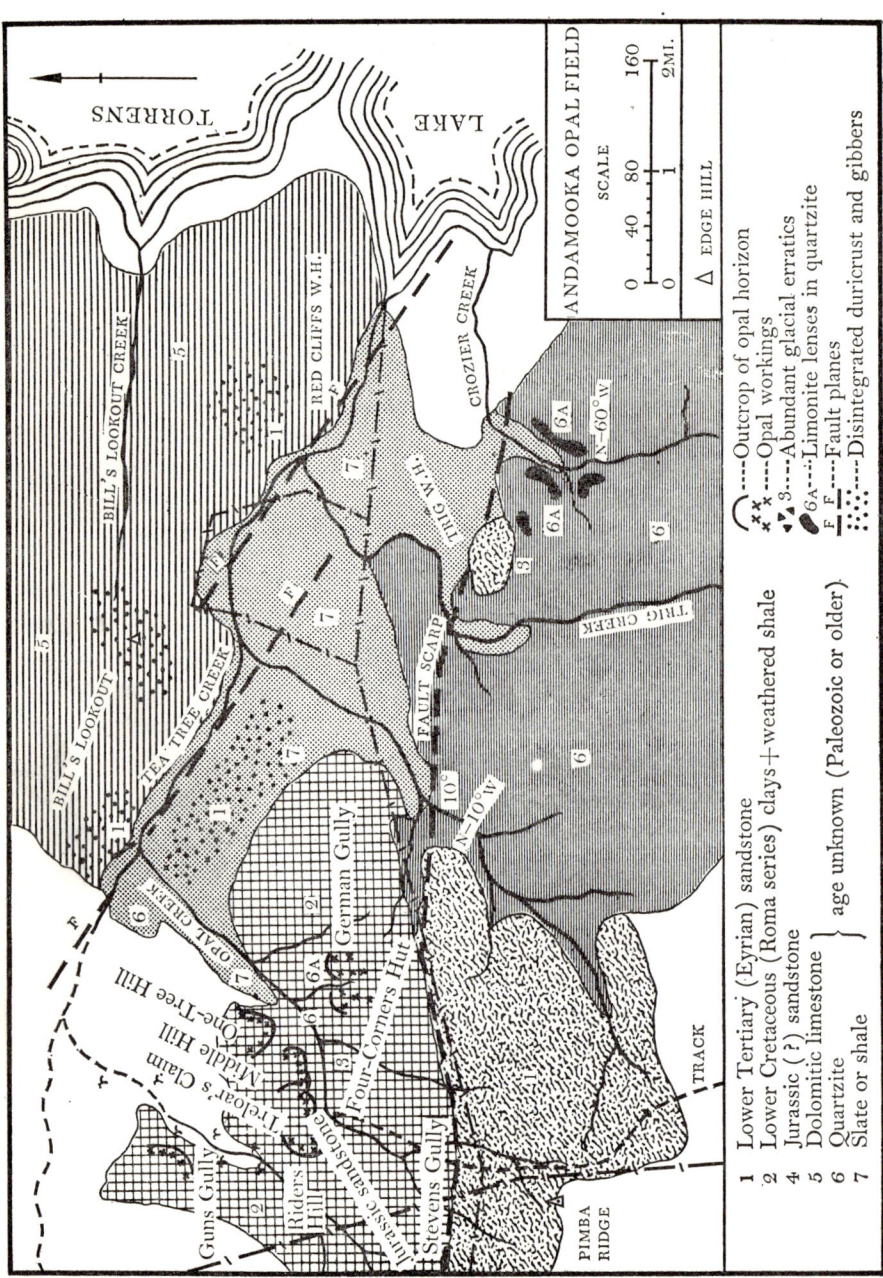

Figure 3: Geological Map of the Anadamooka Opal Field

exposure is 8° W. of N. (magnetic), and the dip is to the east at an angle of 10°. On tracing this bed of quartzite in an easterly direction—that is, downstream along the northern bank of Teatree Creek—the quartzite thins out until the limestone is found to overlap and lie directly upon the purple slates. A good exposure of this overlap exists at Red Cliffs waterhole. Limonite occurs over a wide area in the basal beds of the quartzites. The formation overlying the quartzite consists of a grayish-buff dolomite limestone, which is in part subcrystalline in structure and carries cherty inclusions. Small exposures of these rocks can be seen at intervals on the western part of the tableland mentioned above. To the north of Teatree Creek, however, and extending northward for at least 3 miles, the whole of the country is underlain by these limestones, the thickness of which in this area cannot be determined for lack of any structural data.

This ancient series of rocks has been gently folded into synclines and anticlines. The limestone outcrops noted on the tableland represent the remnants of these rocks preserved in synclines, the anticlinal portions of the beds having been eroded away.

A few yards west of Four Corners Hut, in the bed of Opal Creek, is a shallow opening which has been made in an outcrop of fine, even-grained white felspathic sandstone containing a very small flake of muscovite. This sandstone was passed through whilst sinking a well near the hut, the section in descending order being as follows:

Surface–8 ft.	Alluvium.
8 ft.–11 ft.	White drift sand with flakes of muscovite.
11 ft.–25 ft.	White felspathic sandstone with flakes of muscovite.
25 ft.–27 ft.	Blackish ferruginous sandstone.

27 ft.–53 ft.   Hard purple thin-bedded decomposing quartzite with thin flakes of mica, parallel with and on the bedding planes.

The sandstone occurring between depths of 11 feet and 27 feet is probably of Jurassic age, although no confirmation from paleontological evidence can be adduced. The sequence corresponds with that observed in the region to the westward, where presumably Jurassic sands underlie Lower Cretaceous shales.

On the southern side of a bend of Trig Creek opposite Trig waterhole (5 miles east of the Opal Field) is Trig Bluff, where thin current-bedded purple quartzites (only a few feet in thickness), overlying purple slates, are exposed at the base of the bluff, lying unconformably upon an old eroded surface of the quartzites, and where there is a yellowish and grayish clay carrying small erratics and being about 55 feet in thickness. These boulder clays represent a glacial horizon of the Lower Cretaceous.

A large fragment of fossilized wood in which woody structure has been replaced by chalcedony and also a fragment of an opalized marine fossil were obtained from the workings at Stevens Gully. The formation from which these specimens were obtained is similar in character to beds situated at Stuart's Range and judged by Dr. Whitehouse, the Australian geologist, to be on the horizon of the junction of stages II and III of the Roma Series (Lower Cretaceous). These clays are in turn overlain uncomformably by 20 feet of current-bedded, very ferruginous sandstone and fine grits, characterized by indefinite plant remains which are straplike in their structure. The rock has been partly converted into quartzite and is of Eyrian (Lower Tertiary) age. The superficial cover resting on this formation at the bluff consists principally of whitish and mauve clays with a proportion of water-worn stones of the ancient quartzites, frag-

Andamooka [103

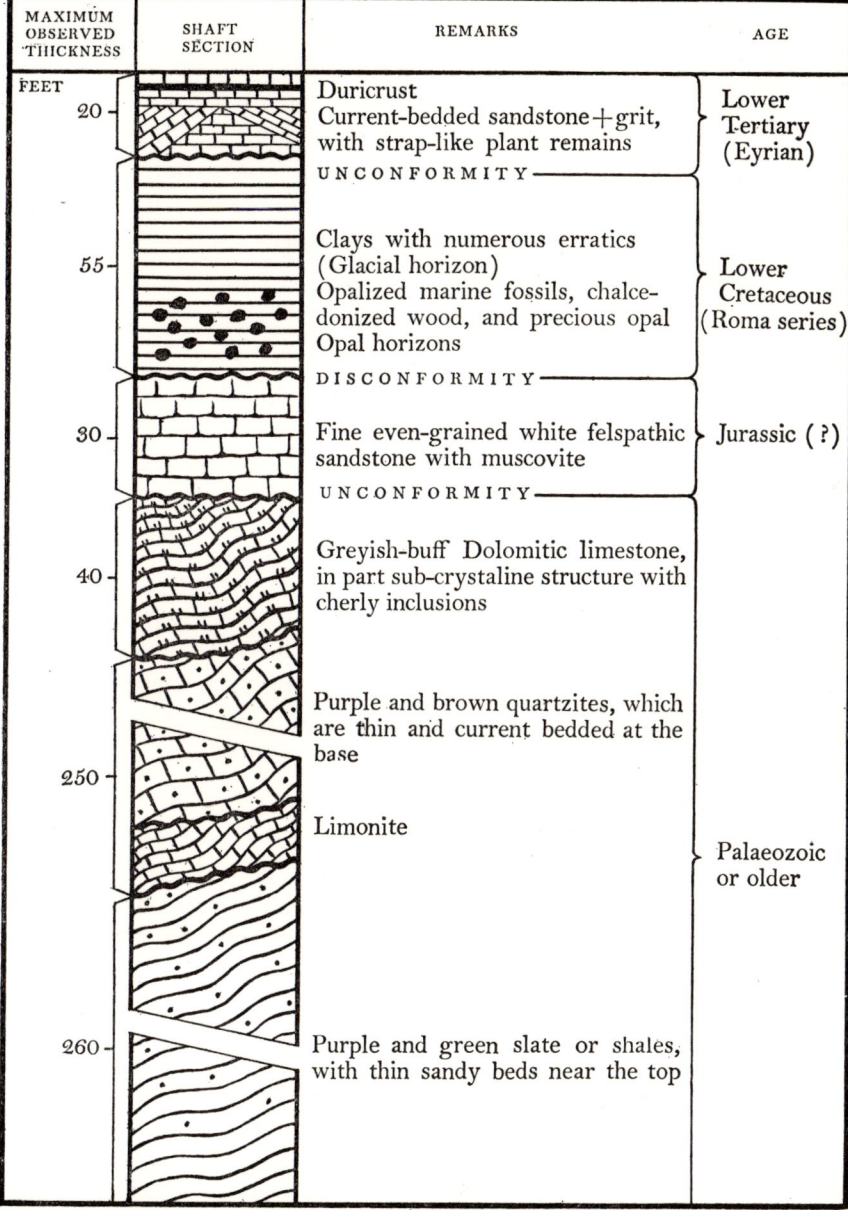

Figure 4: Geological Stratification at Andamooka

ments of chert, from the limestones and quartz. This material has undergone a superficial silicification, making a quartzite crust which also breaks down to form boulders. Isolated outcrops and massive blocks of this siliceous material and numerous boulders occur along both banks of Teatree Creek and over the whole of the tableland and the areas to the north of Teatree Creek, indicating a wide former extension of this formation. Ample evidence was observed in the locality of geological faulting of the ancient and younger formations. Two periods of faulting (and folding referred to) appear to have taken place in the region bordering the western margin of Lake Torrens.

The first period of faulting probably occurred in pre-Eyrian times after the deposition of the Lower Cretaceous sediments, with a subsequent period of faulting, combined with uplift, in post-Eyrian times. Teatree Creek has cut its bed along east-west fault planes. The dolomitic limestone underlying the country to the north of Teatree Creek is resting upon the purple slates, the junction being about 50 feet above the country to the south of Teatree Creek. These structural relations are probably due to an uplift during the second stage of faulting. No trace of any dolomitic limestone was observed south of Teatree Creek except for narrow strips referred to on the high tableland.

Yarloo Creek (south of the tableland), a tributary of Andamooka Creek, has its bed along an east-west fault plane, which can be clearly seen in the bank of the creek by a recent washout above Yarloo Well. Faulting has also occurred farther south, adjacent to a tributary of Andamooka Creek, opposite the homestead, where the ancient quartzites and slates have been steeply folded between parallel fault planes, which are visible in the banks of the creek.

The opal field proper is situated on both sides of Opal Creek and about $2\frac{1}{2}$ miles northeast of Pimba Ridge. The

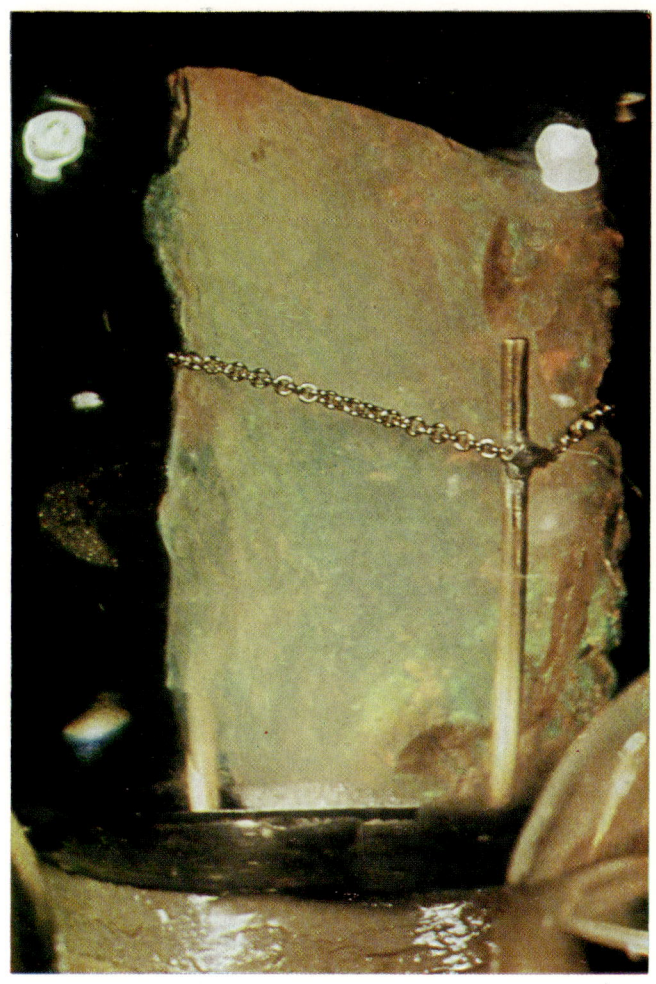

Plate 22: An outstanding large specimen of uncut opal. The chain is for ornamental effect. From Andamooka. (Photo courtesy W. H. Walker.)

Plate 23: A grand assortment of rough specimens from Andamooka.

field covers an area of about 5 square miles, but the actual workings, which are widely scattered over the area mentioned, can be enclosed in an area of about $2\frac{1}{2}$ square miles.

Opal was first discovered accidentally by two boundary riders, Sam Brooks and R. Shepherd, on the hillside of what is now known as "Treloar's Claim" and was identified as precious opal by Bruce M. Foulis (the manager of Andamooka sheep station) on August 29, 1930. The first miners were Mr. Treloar and a boundary rider, P. Evans, who worked on the claim for several months, obtaining opal to the value of about $7,100 before the discovery was generally known. At this time there were as many as 25 miners in the field, whereas in 1935 there were only 14. Today there are 50 or more (including aboriginals).

All the workings consist of shallow shafts, ranging from 2 feet to about 24 feet in depth, the average being from 10 to 12 feet. The shaft is taken down to a characteristic boulder bed in which the opal is found, and the boulders and clay are gouged out for a short distance beyond the shaft itself. A large number of these shafts were examined, and the following geological sequence in descending order can be regarded as being typical of the opal-bearing strata, which are horizontally bedded, passed through. From the surface:

2–5 ft.   Red-brown clay with boulders (surface alluvium). Hard white clay, with very fine grains of sand and horizontal seams of gypsum up to 2 inches in thickness.

9–12 ft.   Tightly packed water-worn boulders of ancient quartzite up to 9 inches diameter, set in a tough white clay, with potch and opal.

6 in.   Ferruginous gypsiferous clay, with a few water-worn boulders and occasional potch and opal.

3–6 ft.   Hard white clay down to the second boulder bed.

The precious opal is obtained principally from a narrow

boulder bed, having a maximum thickness of 2 feet but generally only 12 inches. The water-worn boulders are often found with a thin coating of opal almost completely surrounding the stone. It has been reported that some potch (common opal) was observed in the second boulder bed, but no attempt is now being made to any extent to prospect this lower horizon because of many disappointing results obtained by earlier prospectors.

The major claims are known locally as Treloar's Claim, Middle Hill, One Tree Hill, Boundary Rider's Hill, Stevens Gully, and German Gully. Treloar's Claim, which is the site of the original discovery, is still being worked by the original claimholder. The deepest shaft (near the top of the hill) is 24 feet in depth, with opal in the tightly packed boulder bed. The shafts lower down the slope, and just above the actual outcrop of the opal around the hillside, are very shallow, some openings being on the outcropping bed itself, where it was noticed that the opal occurred principally in the white clay, the opal coated boulders being rare. The workings at Stevens Gully at times were abandoned, but the occurrence of opal on this part of the field is somewhat different from that on the others. The opal zone generally consists of massive angular blocks of ancient quartzite, measuring as much as 2 feet by 2 feet by 1 foot, the water-worn boulders being very scarce. The blocks of quartzite are traversed by fine veins of precious opal, which run across as well as with the bedding planes of quartzite. The veins of opal are of very good color, and range up to one inch in their thickness. At the German Gully workings the best-quality gem is obtained from the thin ferruginous gypsiferous bed immediately below the first or upper opal-bearing boulder bed.

It must be pointed out that, although opal to the value of 25,000 to 30,000 pounds is reported to have been recovered from the time of the discovery in 1935 to 1960, no exact value can be assessed because of the nature of irregular methods of sales. However, it must be assumed that values to the extent of at least 500,000 pounds have been mined to date. The field cannot be regarded as one of unlimited extent. The present workings on most of the claims have proved the extent of the opal-bearing boulder bed in the immediate vicinity, but at German, Stevens, and Guns Gully, and the land in between, the full extent of the opal-bearing bed has not yet been determined.

As the opal-bearing and associated beds are practically horizontally bedded, likely areas to prospect are between German and Stevens Gullies, and also between Stevens Gully and Boundary Rider's Hill, where the opal-bearing boulder bed should outcrop about halfway up the hillsides. It is not expected that the opal zone will extend southward beyond a line drawn through the most southerly workings of German and Stevens Gullies, since these workings are very close to the main east-west fault scarp which bounds the northern edge of the Pimba Ridge tableland.

The miners in the field have experienced considerable difficulty in connection with water and other supplies. These problems as of now have to a great extent been remedied, owing to better roads to the area and more modern transportation. In the early days, water had been drawn from two wells sunk in Opal Creek adjacent to the opal field (before its discovery) by the manager of Andamooka sheep station, and by a shallow well sunk by miners in the same creek about a quarter of a mile downstream from the former two. The miners' well has only been sunk to water level, where the very limited supply of a few bucketfuls of water a day is obtained. The other two wells mentioned each have a yield of about 200 gallons per day, all of which is required by the manager of the station during the summer for the development of the northern part of the run and the watering of stock. The miners will mainly have to search for their own supplies.

The quality of water in the various wells is exceptionally good, and quite suitable for human needs, provided the water is not contaminated by sanitary arrangements, which must be placed downstream from the miners' well. In the early days, there were no supplies whatever in the way of stores on the field; at the present time, there is a store and post office for the convenience of miners.

As of this date, the field still produces, the opal bringing higher prices in the world market and the Japanese buying most of the present-day output. As pointed out, it is not feasible to arrive at the values mined out, but a letter dated February 8, 1960, received from my good friend E. Gregory Sherman, states that he has just arrived back in Sydney from a buying trip to the field, where he purchased opal amounting to $58,500. As has been pointed out, Mr. Sherman makes a trip about once a month to the field and purchases most of the opal offered, which, he also states, is almost entirely sold on his arrival back in Sydney. He also states that the world demand remains exceptionally good. It has also been noted in an earlier chapter that Ernie Sherman, father of E. Gregory Sherman, was an early-day buyer at Lightning Ridge and White Cliffs; his name was as famous as those of Ted Murphy, Percy Marks, and others. His son carries on in the same tradition and is the largest buyer of opal in the world today.

9 Coober Pedy and Tintinbar

COOBER PEDY is situated in the Stuart Range area, 600 miles north northwest from Adelaide, the capital of the state of South Australia, and about 200 miles northwest of Andamooka as the crow flies—and much farther by road. It is approximately 150 miles north of the Trans-Australian Railroad, where a road branches to the north from a place on the map called Kingoonya. The various places marked en route could be very misleading to one not acquainted with or accustomed to Australian maps and travel. Maps show many places that could be mistaken for towns or hamlets—places that, in many cases, are actually homesteads or sheep stations where supplies can always be obtained.

Opal was first discovered at Coober Pedy in 1915 by some prospectors traveling west seeking gold. Their discovery yielded seam or vein opal in an exposed ledge out of which some very fine gem-quality opal has been produced. The location is an extremely desolate one. There is no wood, water, or shade; water is hauled from a source about 20 miles away. Then also, as at Andamooka, the heat, especially during the summer months, is unbearable, with daily temperatures of 115°. The nights, however, are usually cool. Consequently, not very many miners or prospectors want to endure these hardships. But there is no doubt that in time to come, and probably with some government aid, this field will be a good producer and could be worked during the winter season in a manner similar to the mining of many of our desert areas in the United States.

What few hardy miners now work at the field live in

dugouts—rooms dug out of the hillside; even the beds are benches left in the rock itself. Coober Pedy derives its name from this unique type of habitation; it is an aboriginal name meaning a man in a hole. Coober Pedy has a small store with a post office attached, and it too is dug into the hillside. Rainfall is only a few inches a year, and this usually is due to thunderstorms which, when they occur, create out of the entire desert a garden of wildflowers.

Some years ago, one solitary old lady lived at this field, and she sold some grand specimens of opal. Like the opal at Andamooka and at White Cliffs in New South Wales, it is seam opal. Seam opal can always be determined by the matrix surface on each side of the piece. At this field opal occurs from the surface down to a depth of almost 70 feet, and the stratum slopes under a ridge. It occurs usually in thin veins of the finest colors.

A new discovery was made in 1946 by an aboriginal lubra (woman) who worked out opal which she sold for over $5,000. She dug out considerably more later on with the help of her menfolk. Her discovery was over eight miles away from the original discoveries, and the opal ran down from the surface to a depth of about 20 feet. All of this bears out the theory that much more opal will be discovered in years to come at this field.

One of the disadvantages of opal mining at Coober Pedy is that the place is situated far off the beaten track and far removed from habitation and supplies as well as water—much more so than the Andamooka field, which is not far from the established Woomera Bombing and Rocket Base. There is at present in Australia a movement undertaken by the federal government, which is studying a plan to subsidize the prospector and encourage all mining endeavors. If and when this comes to pass, and many miners and prospectors obtain support with funds (grubstaking), it can be expected that other opal discoveries will certainly be made in this promising Coober Pedy area.

I am indebted to the *Australian Bulletin* of November 4, 1961, for the following interesting article entitled "When the Tank Dries Up" from an Adelaide correspondent:

"If you're white you get 20 gallons of water a week at Coober Pedy, the opal field about 400 miles along the track from Port Augusta to Darwin. It has to cover all your washing, drinking and cooking needs. If you're black you get less than half that amount. The 500,000-gallon tank built about 1921, a few years after the first white and black miners began to work the opal field, has not held water since the end of last year. The underground tank, fed by intermittent rains in an area where rain sometimes does not fall for years, is also empty. Last December about 60 men working with seven winches and a bull-dozer removed 18 inches of mud from the tank.

"In the first phase of the crisis water was carted from a brackish bore about 17 miles from the 'township.' But many of the several hundred people living at the field found the water too salty to drink and also hardly good enough to wash with. So water had to be carted over outback tracks a distance of some 80 miles from the McDougall Peak Homestead. Even then a compromise had to be reached. Each two loads of good quality water as late as last month was being mixed with one load of poorer water from nearby.

"Efforts were being made by the Mines Department to find water by the sinking of a bore, but to no avail. Rationing was intensified. This week the Australian Labor Party Opposition back-bencher, Mr. Loveday (Whyalla District), told the House of Assembly that he had received reports on Coober Pedy. One was that 70 aborigines had left the opal field, and another, from the secretary of the local progress association at Coober Pedy, confirmed that the water ration had been cut. Mr. Loveday asked if the 70 aborigines who had just left Coober Pedy were the same as those who arrived recently in a walkabout party from the Yalata Mission station several hundred miles away, and if any undue pressure had been placed on them to leave the area.

"The Minister in charge of Native Welfare, Mr. Glen Pearson, confirmed that the natives who left Coober Pedy did come from the Mission Station, but he said a local native welfare officer had merely 'persuaded' a number of natives to leave the field.

"If it is true that natives regularly employed at the field had been asked to leave, it would seem to be discrimination against native workers, since there are no reports of permanent white workers being asked to leave. To many aborigines there is little difference between a white man's order and a white man's request. So it will be a matter of opinion whether there has been undue pressure.

"The ironical part of the story is that the water supply position has been aggravated by whites themselves. The population has increased nearly twofold in recent months. Both black and white miners, without jobs because of the recent economic cutbacks, have landed at the field with hardly the price of a return fare but plenty of hopes to strike it rich quickly and get out. (The problem has been aggravated also by motorists who have relied upon the settlement in the past to restock their own depleted water canteens.) The mere fact that more than 500,000 pounds ($1,125,000) worth of opal is now won from Coober Pedy and South Australia's other major field, Andamooka, annually is enough to ensure that population troubles will continue."

The little-known field of Tintinbar is situated between the towns of Ballina and Lismore out toward the coast in northern New South Wales and only a short distance south of the Queensland border. One peculiar thing about the field

Plate 24: Some typical miners' habitations at Coober Pedy.

is that it is out of the sedimentary regions, being located in an igneous area, and the opal there is found in basalt, an igneous rock. An interesting fact also is that its location is several hundreds of miles from Lightning Ridge, which is a sedimentary area and is to the west. Opal found at Tintinbar is very beautiful: light colors as well as black, a great amount of it being almost transparent—a jelly type having very fine color flashes. This opal, in its characteristics, resembles the opal from Rainbow Ridge in Nevada. It has a large water content, in some cases as much as 12 percent. At deeper levels it has a lesser water content, a fact for which there is no explanation.

At present there is no mining activity at this field, since opal with such a great water content is very unstable and, on exposure to the atmosphere, will crack with a spider-web appearance. Therefore it is useless as a gem stone. This opal is the only opal in Australia that contains so much water. The opal from all the other sources is very durable and has a very low water content.

I have never visited the field at Tintinbar, but I have observed specimens from there on display at the Mining Museum in Sydney. Like the mining people at the Nevada location, various authorities in Australia have tried many methods which they thought might tend to eliminate the cracking of the opal on its exposure—all without any successful results.

10 Rainbow Ridge

RAINBOW RIDGE is situated in the Virgin Valley area in the northwest corner of the state of Nevada, in Humboldt County. It is about halfway between the small settlement of Denio on the Oregon-Nevada border and Cedarville near the California border to the west. It is reached by reasonably good roads. Whoever named the area Virgin Valley had a realistic vision of the desert area, for the name is appropriate in every respect. In that sense it has much in common with Coober Pedy and Andamooka in Australia, although it is much more accessible, owing to improved roads.

The opal there was first discovered in 1905 by a cowhand named James Flinders who was riding the range and was employed by the land barons Miller and Lux, who controlled hundreds of square miles of territory for cattle and sheep grazing. This first discovery was some opalized wood float on the top of the ridge where the mine stands today. Since opal at this period was being given much publicity in the Australian fields, this discovery naturally caused considerable interest.

When the discovery was first made, it was only natural that Flinders and others did not know what it was. A specimen was forwarded to Reno, where it was identified as opal pseudomorph after wood. The area was prospected, and a few hardy, adventurous individuals arrived. There never were a great many who stayed. This probably was for several reasons, one being that supplies were obtained from a considerable distance, and roads at the time were extremely bad. Water is to be had close by in plentiful supply, but the climate is very unpredictable. In the summer it is extremely hot, and the winters are long and cold, with temperatures reaching as low as 30° below zero.

It was during this period of much publicity that the San Francisco newspaper the *Call* sent Mrs. F. H. Lockheed to the location to make a report on it for the paper. She was so impressed with what she saw that she stayed. Since the discovery was on government grazing land, she experienced little trouble in obtaining mining rights. She was a remarkable woman. She supervised her mining operations and worked with her men. The opal here is unsurpassed for its grand color by any in the world. But as it contains as much as eleven percent of water, it is very unstable for gems and has the tendency to craze and fracture after being mined and exposed to the atmosphere. Specimens are very outstanding for their breath-taking beauty and are in constant demand by the collectors and museums, who are more than willing to pay big prices for them.

At the ridge a tunnel was driven from one side to the other; this was started by Mrs. Lockheed, whose engineering was extremely good, for as the tunnel was dug from either end, it was out of line by only a few inches when it reached the center. Years ago the author observed freshly mined refuse opal which had been exposed on the dumps to the hot sun crack and crumble away.

Geologically, the general area is mainly igneous, with series of sedimentary depositions; it is in these sedimentary areas that the opal exists, both at Rainbow Ridge and also in the large veins of common opal a few miles distant from the ridge. The material in the main tunnel at the mine consists of a hard-packed clay, which contains many semipetrified small limbs, twigs, and swamp rushes. No fossils have been discovered. When it was found that the opal was not

[120] The Book of Opals

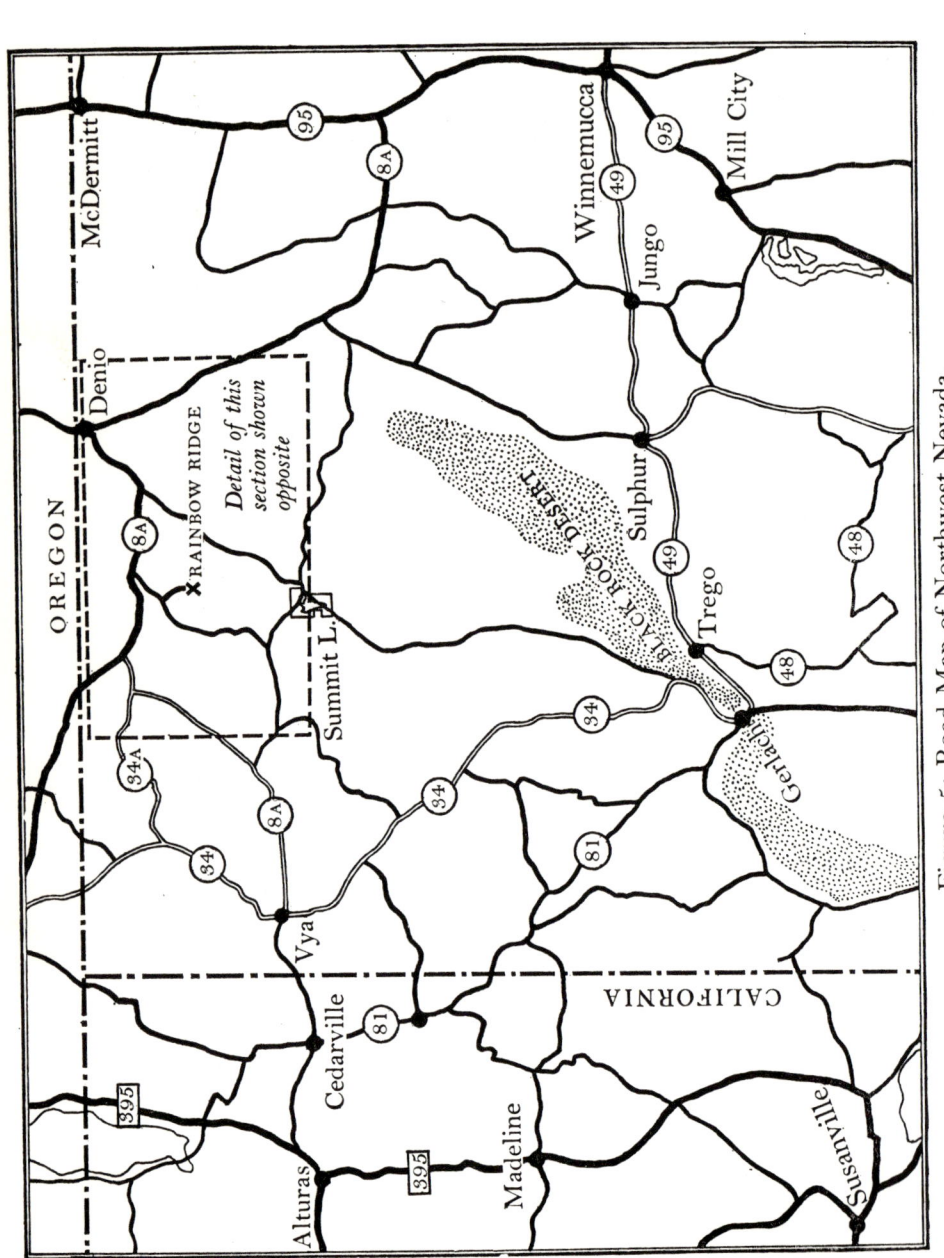

Figure 5: Road Map of Northwest Nevada,

Rainbow Ridge [121]

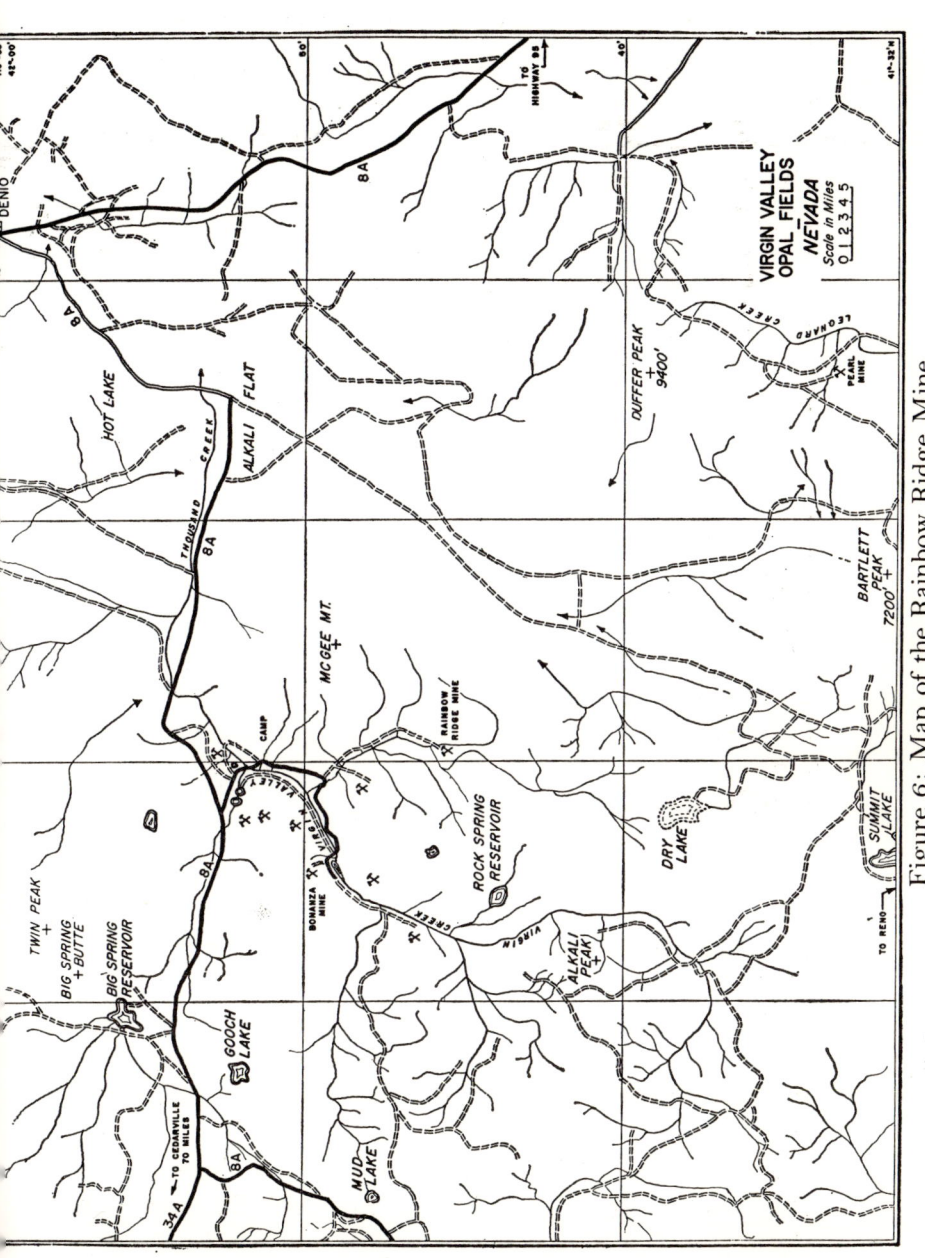

Figure 6: Map of the Rainbow Ridge Mine

suitable for gems, Mrs. Lockheed turned her interests over to the Hammond Company of Santa Barbara, California. Shortly after this period the United States Wildlife Refuge Agency took over the area. This did not affect the mining rights, so today it is situated in what is known as the Sheldon National Antelope Reserve. Visitors and prospectors are warned not to carry firearms. Considerable prospecting is still carried on each summer, and a few isolated spots have produced some opal, but not much of importance has yet been discovered. One other very outstanding discovery was made a few miles distant from Rainbow Ridge. This proved to be an opalized tree section. It was not a mine and was only a few feet under the surface in volcanic ash. It was trenched, and some grand opal was obtained from it. It was given the name of the Bonanza, but it proved to be only a localized enrichment.

In the early days of operation much carelessness prevailed, and a great amount of opal was stolen or "highgraded"—how much, no one will ever know. It was discovered that the southern end of the ridge contained the most opal, and a drift from the main tunnel was developed and the entire southern end worked through a series of connecting rooms, leaving pillars to support the roof. Here in this section many beautiful pieces were obtained, and on one occasion a five-gallon kerosene can almost full of opal was left overnight in the tunnel. In the morning it was gone, and so were a couple of the men. One of these men was known as Opal Shorty; what his true name was, no one ever knew. Since they had a considerable start, they were hard to follow, but they were traced as far east as Salt Lake City in Utah, where their trail ended.

Soon after this, it was announced that Colonel W. A. Roebling, of Brooklyn Bridge and wire-cable fame, had purchased the world's finest black opal specimen for $75,000 (some say it was $50,000; the exact price is not known, nor was it ever disclosed). It weighed 16.95 ounces. The name of the man who sold this specimen to the colonel was also never disclosed. Since Mrs. Lockheed was operating the mine at the time, I asked her if it was she who had made the sale. She stated that she knew nothing of the transaction. Later, Colonel Roebling presented the specimen to the Smithsonian Institution, the United States National Museum in Washington, D. C., where it is now on public exhibit. I should mention that Opal Shorty died a few years ago in the town of Winnemucca, Nevada. Mrs. Lockheed passed away around 1950 in Los Angeles, where several of her relatives still live.

A great amount of common opal also exists in the area, and most of this is highly fluorescent. This opal is of a light translucent greenish color. It is situated in a large deposit of diatomaceous earth, and a vein of eight to ten inches extends under the body for some distance. Also in this same vicinity is common opal of a canary-yellow color, streaked with black, possibly a manganese stain. Both of these are in considerable demand as specimens, one for its fluorescence, the other for its color.

During the depression of the 1930's the government established a C.C.C. camp about eight miles from the Rainbow Ridge mine. One Saturday night some of these boys entered the tunnel to highgrade some opal. Since there were no timbers, and the formation was of a clay which crumbles because of air circulating from the one end of the tunnel to the other, these workings were extremely dangerous, especially to those without mining experience. A cave-in occurred, and two of the boys were killed. Although the mine is situated in a very lonely and isolated place, with no habitation for many miles, highgraders were not deterred. At one time I was working there with Mark Foster, the caretaker. After mining all day, Mark would insist that we remove our tools. When I asked why, he said that highgraders would park their cars a couple of miles away, walk to the mine after dark, and sometimes use the tools that had been left there. The reason they parked so far away was that a car can be heard a great distance away in the lonely stillness. Saturday nights were the highgraders' favorite times to work. So on a Saturday night Mark would borrow my gun, and, with a flashlight, we would stealthily enter the tunnel; but luckily for the highgraders, none were encountered while I was present, although on one occasion I observed tailings they had left after a night's work.

The mine at the present time is owned and operated by my good friend Keith Hodson, who is carrying on in the footsteps of his recently deceased father, Glen Hodson. Together they installed much modern equipment, and some very fine material is still obtained from the mine. Not long before the senior Hodson's death, they unearthed an even larger opal specimen than the one on exhibit at the Smithsonian Institution. It is a wood replacement of the same caliber. The Hodsons exhibited this specimen at many gem and mineral conventions.

As for any future discovery of opal in the region, it is extremely doubtful, since, over the last thirty years, the entire region of at least fifty square miles has been painstakingly prospected by hundreds of geologists, mineralogists, and professional and amateur rock hounds every summer. This is not to say that opal does not exist in this region. I emphasize only that it is doubtful that, after such extensive prospecting, any more will be discovered. It has to be remembered that the original discovery at Rainbow Ridge was through some surface float and that, if any surface float existed anywhere in the area, by now it would certainly have been discovered. So if opal does exist, it is covered by over-

Plate 25: The owner of the Rainbow Ridge Mine working a drift.

Plate 26: The main tunnel of the Rainbow Ridge Mine.

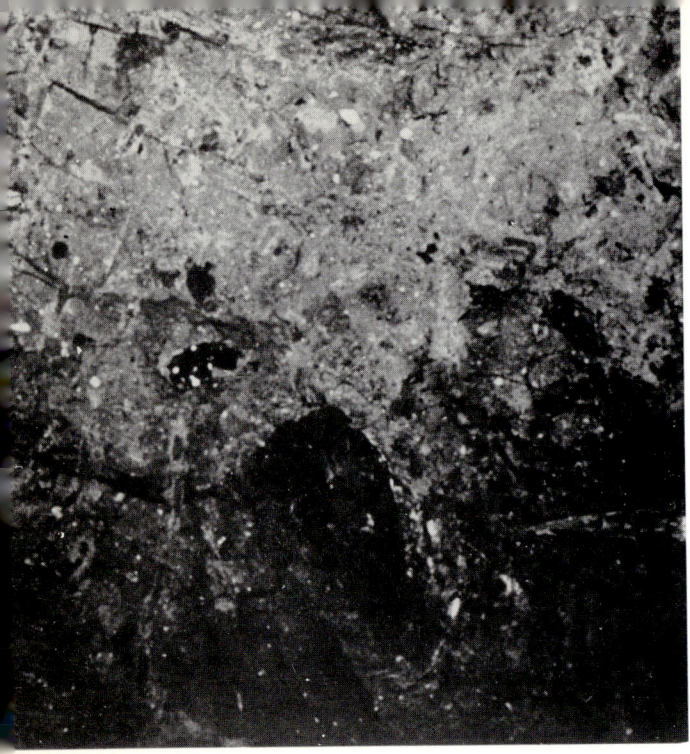

Plate 27: A section of the wall rock of the Rainbow Ridge Mine. Note encrusted opals at lower center of photo. The tip of the pick, showing at bottom right, indicates the size of the stones.

Plate 28: Keith Hodson mining for opal in one of the drifts at Rainbow Ridge.

burden, and under this condition it is not going to be uncovered without some indication on the surface.

One very peculiar circumstance was observed at the Rainbow Ridge mine. This was that the opal was not generally dispersed throughout the formation but was rather only at about eye-level height in the tunnel. Below and above, no opal existed. The tunnel driven from the west side of the ridge was absolutely devoid of any opal for at least 100 feet. Along with Mark Foster, I made a drift from about the center of the main tunnel to the northeast, and all opal found in this drift existed at eye level only, becoming entirely played out after 20 feet of drifting. No seam or vein opal existed at the Rainbow Ridge mine; all opal was in individual pieces embedded in the hard-packed sedimentary formation. This condition is similar in some ways to that at Lightning Ridge, in Australia, where small individual opal in a nodular form is found in the clay formation underlying the siliceous formation above it. A very much different situation in reference to the above is found at both Andamooka and Coober Pedy in South Australia; here all the opal is in seam or vein deposits, mainly attached to the hard siliceous formation.

Any talk of the area would not be complete without mentioning that in the early days there was situated in Virgin Valley the Virgin Ranch. This lonely ranch was about eight miles distant from the Rainbow Ridge mine and was operated by Dan Archevelita and his wife, people of Basque nationality. The ranch was stocked with sheep. The Archevelitas often took care of stranded miners who, having no direct sale for their opal and being unable to obtain food supplies except from a great distance, presented their opals to Mrs. Archevelita, who at one time had a remarkable collection of representative specimens.

It was around 1935 that the United States wildlife authorities took over the entire area, which is now known as the Sheldon Antelope Refuge. I happened to be in the area the very day that Dan Archevelita was evacuating with his herd, covered wagons, chuck wagon, and hired hands, driving his stock over 100 miles to the east near Winnemucca, where he was to make a new start with another homestead.

If one visits the region today, he will observe that the government has set up very extensive and picturesque headquarters on the main road about halfway between Denio on the Nevada-Oregon border and Cedarville, California. Herds of antelope can be seen grazing without fear of intruders. Since it is a game refuge, firearms are banned, and coyotes just sit up and, knowing they will not be molested, act cheeky. Many other wild denizens also abound, and one will be fortunate if he does not encounter some rattlesnakes, for they too are not uncommon.

The present owner and operator of the mine, as I have already noted, is my good friend Keith Hodson, a graduate of the School of Mines at Socorro, New Mexico, and a very capable mining man. He also owns and operates several turquoise properties in Nevada and maintains a fine gem and mineral establishment at Scottsdale, Arizona. His father, the late Glen Hodson, after obtaining possession of the mine at Rainbow Ridge, built a fine residence, installed electricity, and, with much modern mining equipment, unearthed considerable fine opal. Keith now carries on at the mine. During the summer months many hundreds of amateur prospectors and members of various mineral and gem societies throughout the United States visit the area. Like his father, Keith always has a welcome for these visitors and allows them to comb the dumps, where it is not unusual to find some choice overlooked opal.

The last time I had the good fortune to meet up with that remarkable lady, Mrs. Lockheed, was in the late summer of 1941. Mark Foster, then caretaker of the mine, and I, after having worked all day in the mine, had had dinner and were enjoying a smoke, sitting outside the cabin in the cool of the evening.

I said: "Mark, I think I hear a car." In that region of stillness a car can be heard as far off as ten miles. Mark listened and agreed that what we heard was a car. In ten or fifteen minutes, around the bend there hove into view a taxicab.

The driver stopped at the cabin, and out stepped a fashionably dressed old lady. Immediately we recognized her as Mrs. Lockheed, the queen of the Rainbow Ridge opal field. Her very first words on alighting were "Mark Foster, what are you doing here?"

"Taking care of the mine, Mrs. Lockheed," Mark replied.

She answered that with "You are stealing all my opals."

Mark assured her that all the opals were safe, but she was hard to convince. At this point she paid off the taxi driver, who had driven her all the way from Los Angeles, a distance of over 700 miles. The taxi driver then put his cab into gear and pressed down hard on the throttle, the rear wheels throwing up a barrage of rocks in the wake of his fast getaway, probably his happy way of bidding us all goodbye.

Mark was now saddled with making his new guest as comfortable as possible, all of which was no great effort. Mark had no bed or privacy; he slept on the dirt floor on an old mattress, but this he gave up for the lady. I had a bunk out in my truck. I gave Mark some spare blankets and he bedded down in a corner on the dirt floor with his clothes on, Indian fashion.

The cooking also was very primitive and not far removed from Indian style, either; it was accomplished on an ancient stove, one left behind by Dan Archevelita over at the Virgin

Ranch house. Fuel was sagebrush, none other being available. I happened to have on hand a goodly supply of canned food out in my truck, so food for the time being was no problem. Mrs. Lockheed seemed to take on a more happy disposition after taking several tours of inspection of the mine and was also more trustful of Mark, for fewer brickbats were coming his way.

On the second day of this disruption, I told Mark that I could not see how this association could continue, since it was such a desert roughing-it life for the old lady, who made herself right at home under the most primitive conditions imaginable. Mark had at times tried to get her to disclose her present address, but all he would get for his efforts was "It's none of your business, Mark Foster." But Mark all this time was doing considerable thinking, and he slyly hit upon a plan. At a moment when the old lady was caught somewhat off guard and in a jovial mood, Mark said: "Say, Mrs. Lockheed, if anything happened to us away out here, would'nt it be awful?" She agreed it certainly would be. Mark then said: "Tell you what I suggest. Let's exchange addresses, so one or the other could call for help." She then gave him her Los Angeles address.

Next morning Mark, under the pretext of going for food and other supplies, drove to the nearest outpost of Denio, 55 miles to the north up on the Oregon border; there he posted a letter to the address given him. Another three days elapsed, and a large modern limousine arrived just as we were all finishing supper. Out stepped a well-dressed city gentleman.

His first words were "Mother, what are you doing here?" Her answer was "Son, what are you doing here?" In a short time she was bundled up into the big limousine, and a very happy goodbye was exchanged, with Mark receiving a $50 bill for his kindness in taking care of Mother. Her son is head of the nationally known company which markets the Lockheed brake fluid, probably used by motorists the whole world over and sold everywhere.

In the summer of 1935, John Melhase, geologist for the Southern Pacific Railroad and my field trip companion, was given an assignment by a large English mining corporation to make a report for them on the Rainbow Ridge property. We were accompanied by an outstanding mining engineer, Chester A. Anderson, whose father was the consulting mining engineer for the Anaconda Mining Company, one of the largest mining companies in the United States. We left Oakland, California, where Anderson resided, and arrived at Virgin Valley the next day, staying overnight en route at Cedarville on the California-Nevada border.

Melhase had visited the mine and the surrounding area a few times previously. Anderson and I had also visited the property before. We made camp near water where today a game warden resides in a stone structure eight miles north of the mine. For almost a whole week the area was prospected. During this time we observed quite a number of prospect holes dug into every patch of volcanic ash by former prospectors in their search for opal. We failed to find any of these showing any indication of opal, outside of the lone locality known as the Bonanza, which has been mentioned previously. The patches of volcanic ash were in the main small in area, situated among much float which consisted chiefly of boulders of andesite. No continuity or definite formation existed, but the general structure, as in most desert areas, was mainly conglomerates.

Melhase was acquainted with the general geological structure of the mine, which was readily determined by examination of the tunnel from one end to the other, a distance of approximately 250 feet. Where opal was encountered, it existed in the clay body which is deposited for some distance inside the tunnel. But not all of this clay contained opal, a considerable area being absolutely barren.

In the early days the only building was a shanty constructed from the local rocks, and these rocks had much space between them, so it was a fine place for rattlesnakes to hide in and keep cool. Outside and adjoining this shanty was a rock wall about four feet high; it served no purpose whatever and appeared to be an unfinished project.

One very hot evening after our party—which consisted of Chester Anderson, Carl (Cappy) Ricks, the caretaker Mark Foster, and I—had finished supper, Anderson went outside and there was greeted by a large and disrespectful rattlesnake, which was in a most angry mood. The rest of the party went out to see what all the fuss was about. When Mr. Rattlesnake observed that he was outnumbered, he decided it was time to crawl into this rock wall. Mark Foster, dancing like a Hopi Indian at the snake dance, ran off somewhere and returned with a length of water pipe, but the snake decided to stay inside, seeking safety.

It was then that Mark hit upon a noble scheme. He went into the cabin and returned with a gallon of gasoline. "This will flush him out," said Mark, pouring the gasoline over the top of the wall. We stood back while a lighted match was tossed at the wall. The following explosion almost knocked all of us over. After the dust had cleared, we all looked for the snake, but he is probably still inside that wall, if it is still standing.

Mark Foster was a very good-natured type of desert rat, but when angered, which was rarely, he could be a very rough individual. One fine Sunday morning a car drove up and parked over on the mine dump, which was four or five hundred yards distant from the cabin. All of us waited to greet the strangers, but instead of coming over to say hello, which is the usual custom, they got their tools from the car and walked around the ridge to the rear entrance of the mine. I was washing up the breakfast dishes when Mark, getting more angry by the minute, approached me and said: "Where is your gun?" I handed him the gun and asked what he was going to do. He replied: "Those two fellows have gone to the back entrance of the mine."

In a few minutes he was lost to sight around the end of the ridge. He soon reappeared with the two gents, who at one time might have been in the army, for they were marching in single file with Mark behind, swinging the gun and loudly shouting: "Another word out of you and I'll fill you both full of lead!" We could hear him plainly over at the cabin, and he certainly meant it. They got back into their car and departed; they probably never knew just how lucky they were.

When Mark arrived back, I asked what had happened. He said that when he accosted them and told them he was in charge, they told him that he had no authority. He then told them he was going to show them some authority, and he certainly did.

As our party was soon leaving for Winnemucca, my friends were very jumpy and nervous; they asked me what would have happened if Mark had shot those men. I consoled them by saying that nothing would have happened except that we would have had to make a call and see the sheriff in Winnemucca to tell him to go out and pick them up, and no further questions would have been asked or needed.

11 Querétaro and Some Minor Localities

QUERÉTARO is situated almost in the center of Mexico and in the state of the same name. The city has a population of 50,000 and is 160 miles northwest of Mexico City. The elevation is 6,000 feet, and a very moderate climate prevails the year round. Here opal has been mined by the Indians for at least a century. Unlike the Australian fields, where opal is obtained from the sedimentary area, at Querétaro the opal is mined from an igneous formation, being embedded in rhyolite. The mining could be termed quarrying rather than mining. The opal is close to the surface, and owing to the very hard, compact rhyolite, the only tools used are small bars, hammers, and picks. Some of the opal is very fine in its quality and color, but not a great amount is obtained for high-priced gem purposes, for in extracting it from the rhyolite, it is invariably fractured, since the rhyolite is much harder than the opal.

Here also is a distinctive type of stone called cherry opal. This gem ranges in color from a clear citrine to a darker red but usually has no play of vivid colors. Local townspeople cut and polish these stones and sell them to visiting tourists. These shop people also have on hand and for sale specimen pieces showing vivid-colored opal embedded in the rhyolite matrix.

The mines are a few miles out of town and are easily accessible. They are situated in a barren area, the vegetation being mainly scrub and cactus. The people, including the miners, are very courteous and friendly and go out of their way to make the visitor welcome. If one does not speak the

Figure 7: Map of Mexico and Central America

language, then guides can be obtained who speak English and are only too glad to escort the visitor to the mines. During the last few years, because of newly built excellent roads, there has been a great influx of American tourists and amateur gem cutters from the many hundreds of gem and mineral societies visiting Querétaro. Even under these conditions the visitor can still obtain some opal, but no longer is anything worthwhile cheap. If one is fortunate in obtaining a gem without the rhyolite matrix attached, such an opal compares with any found elsewhere. Recently a good friend who has the incentive to be always on the lookout for bargains and for what can be termed "sleepers" visited the Mexican government pawnshop, the *monte de piedad* (meaning the "house of pity"), in Mexico City. Here he found for sale the finest Querétaro opal it has been my good fortune ever to view. This opal, cut as a cabochon of at least 20 carats and set in a 14-carat heavy gold ring, he purchased for only $40 in United States currency. I offered him $500 for it, and all I received was a laugh.

The translucent cherry opals, usually of one to two carats, are rather plentiful, and these do not have any of the rhyolite matrix adhering to them. They are sold rather cheaply: as low as a few cents each. This type is the only variety of opal that can be successfully faceted, but faceting does not enhance its beauty in any way.

There are numerous other locations adjacent to Querétaro where some opal has been found, but no area other than Querétaro has produced anything in the way of commercial value; so we need not mention these.

Mexico is a very heavily populated country, and the masses live on a very low income. Regardless of this, one will find the people seemingly happy. Quite a number make their living by either mining, cutting, or selling opal. Very little of the opal from Querétaro finds its way abroad; most of it is sold at its place of origin. It seems that tourists and other visitors absorb the entire production, whether it is opal of gem quality or opal matrix specimens.

Hotel accommodations are of a high standard, and prices for these, as well as for food, are about half of what one would be charged in the United States. The visitor to Querétaro, as well as other sections in Mexico, is warned to drink only bottled waters or water which hotels all supply the guest with for drinking purposes; water drunk with undue care will certainly produce intestinal effects and cause much discomfort and spoil a vacation and visit. I once experienced this discomfort. Ordering pineapple juice one morning at breakfast which was cooled with ice cubes evidently made from the local water confined me to bed for four days.

It has been my intention only to elaborate upon the most prominent opal fields that have world-renowned significance and have produced opal in a commercial way, whether the opal was mined for its gem value or for its museum or specimen value. With regard to the few isolated discoveries of opal, none of these are outstanding, and there is little in the way of interest to report about them, outside of passing comment.

From time to time there have been random or isolated discoveries. For instance, in the vicinity of the town of Moscow, Idaho, there are at least several of these; however, none have produced in a commercial way. There are two locations in the state of Oregon, one at Opal Butte and another at Heppner in the center of the state. At these locations someone at times finds a stray opal. In California, at Zabriskie Point, near Shoshone, Inyo County, small pinfire specks are found in a crumbly silicified clay. Another location in California where an odd gemmy opal has been found is Red Rock Canyon in Kern County. But neither of these locations has produced anything outside of a stray piece or two. Since all of the above-mentioned locations are in igneous areas consisting of rhyolite, trachyte, basalt, etc., they are not conducive to the production of opal in a commercial manner.

Some authorities have mentioned that opal of gem quality is to be found in Honduras. I am convinced that this Honduran locality is not very productive. The reason for this view is the fact that, in my experience, where any gem or mineral exists it is exploited, and to the fullest—this regardless of wherever in the world it exists. Although I do not dispute the existence of opal in Honduras, there are one or two questions I should like to ask: How much? To what extent? It is to be reasoned that if precious opal existed to any extent it certainly would be in general circulation.

Having made extensive inquiry regarding this location of opal, I have been unable to find any great source of it outside of the mention of odd pieces. The opal is stated to be of sev-

Figure 8: Map of the Opal Fields of Honduras

eral types and all of fine quality, supposedly even better than the best from Querétaro. This I doubt. It has also been stated that, for a time, there was produced opal of the same type and quality as the now extinct Hungarian opal. It is further stated that much common opal as well as a cherry opal like that from Mexico is obtained, together with a quantity of hyalite opal (the glass-clear variety).

The Smithsonian Institution states that Honduras is known as a locality for precious opal, and the locality is briefly described in some gem books. These advise me that no large quantities of the gem have ever been produced in Honduras. They also advise that the Smithsonian Institution's collection contains only two pieces, one labeled simply "Honduras" and the other with the indication that the piece came from near Erandique, Department of Gracias. Neither specimen, as I have noted earlier, is on public exhibit.

Mr. G. F. Claringbull, curator of mineralogy at the British Museum, advises me that the museum has specimens of precious as well as common opal from Honduras. The two principal locations from which these come are Gracias a Dios and Erandique. The precious opals are very transparent (hydrophane) or milky, and some of them have a good play of color. The only specimen on exhibit is a nodule of precious opal in rhyolite. Most of these specimens have been in the museum's collection a great many years, in some cases for more than a century.

There are a great many of these insignificant locations in many areas throughout Australia, especially in the state of Queensland. After considerable development of many of these locations they have not produced anything worthwhile in a commercial way.

12 The Opal Trade

THE PURCHASING of opal in its rough, newly mined state can be a very uncertain transaction. The jeweler buys his opal gems already cut and either mounted or ready to mount. Collectors, lapidaries, amateurs, and professionals usually wish to purchase the rough material so as to fashion their own gems from it. A great many, in doing so, usually experience considerable disappointment—mainly, I believe, because they do not understand the opal or the method by which miners and opal dealers operate. The miner who has been fortunate, probably after months of hard work, is not going to give his hard-won values away. He usually has a valuator and appraiser in the field who will give him advice as to the quality and value of his opal. Each and every piece and fragment is snipped in his appraisal so as to observe the colors. The appraiser is rewarded for his work by receiving a percentage of the value. Anyone laboring under the impression that the appraiser has overlooked something should change his view.

The miner now has his sale price, and it will rarely be altered or, especially, lowered. This price is usually accepted by the opal buyer arriving in the field from the city, and he in turn receives orders for rough opal from local as well as foreign cutters. For instance, an order states a request for 10 ounces of opal at $5 or even $10 per ounce. The opal dealer has this grade in stock and also in a price range up to $250 an ounce or over. He also has in stock cut stones from 2 up to 20 carats which bring from $10 a carat to perhaps $100 a carat and over. When the dealer purchases the parcel of opal from the miner, all of the opal from the strike is in the parcel, and there are many pieces that are absolutely devoid of any color to speak of—pieces that are probably little better than common opal. When the dealer in turn receives the order for opal, he places his hand into the small (usually cotton) bag containing this particular price range and grade, and, with no picking or selecting, places exactly 10 ounces troy on his scale.

I can state that out of every four ounces, at least one ounce will be practically worthless. The dealer is really not responsible for this method, for he had to purchase the parcel that way himself. Naturally when the purchaser receives his shipment he is somewhat disappointed to find some pieces that are practically worthless included in it. But as a rule enough good values prevail, especially if good judgment is efficiently used in the fashioning of it into gem stones. This will more than offset and compensate for the useless material. One may ask: "Why doesn't the dealer sort out only the good material anyway?" He probably would comply with this request, but instead of the price being, say, $10 per ounce, it may be raised to $15 per ounce. Cut gems, including doublets (two-piece opals), are at times sold by the individual stone, but the stone already has been weighed and the price determined by the carat for that particular quality. All cut stones are always sold by the carat weight and rough opal by the troy-ounce weight.

I believe that I am very conversant with any opal trade in the United States, and I can honestly state that the opal market here is indeed poor compared with trade and prices in other lands. Opals in London, Paris, Berlin, and Tokyo have a more ready sale and sell at higher prices. It appears that for some unaccountable reason opal for sale in many United States stores is of poor grade, being mostly white, almost colorless opal. However, prices charged for this type of stone are altogether unreasonable. If one searches far enough, he can find an odd, nice gem exhibited for sale, but it is rare, and even the selection will be limited indeed, whereas in Europe and Australia it is not uncommon to find jewelry stores with a large assortment of fine, high-priced gems.

Another distressing feature is the fact that many gem cutters and many jewelry stores are under the impression that opal is a cheap product. How far wrong can they be? As an opal cutter and dealer, I have had, in my time, the opportunity to meet thousands who wished to purchase opal. These, in a great many cases, have been amateur cutters, rock hounds, gem collectors, and even some professional lapidaries. All have been stunned when confronted with and offered a really outstanding gem, such a gem weighing from 10 to 15 carats and selling at a price of $400 to $500, which is the price that an unusual gem will command—and in some cases very much more.

Many of these people stated that they desired rough opal of the type of such a gem and were prepared to pay somewhere from $5 to $20 an ounce. Mind you, per ounce—not having any particle of understanding that such gem material is never sold by the ounce even if it was mined in that manner, which it rarely is. It is sold only by the carat. Perhaps some of this misunderstanding lies in the fact that the white, opaque milk opal (mainly poorly colored), which is itself not what one could term too plentiful, is offered in ounce quantities by both the miners and the opal dealers.

This brings us to the question: "Is opal scarce?"

I have been asked this question a great many times, and the answer is both no and yes. The white milk opal, which is opaque and usually contains a play of red color—commonly in bands—is very plentiful and rather cheap. Normally it is sold in its rough state by the ounce, the price ranging from $2 to $10 per ounce. The higher-priced gem opal, which is mined at all fields, is never sold by the ounce. This type of precious opal is sold only by the carat. Most of it is cut right in Australia for the trade, so it is never overplentiful. Tourists traveling from near and far, ships' crews, airline crews and passengers, businessmen and their wives—all seem to be well aware of the fact that Australia produces opals, just as one would be aware that South Africa produces diamonds.

The visitor to Australia can purchase rough opal but usually only the cheaper grades, for, as we have pointed out, the high-priced material is mostly cut there for the jewelry trade and is then usually sold in mounted jewelry. Tourists and other visitors almost all purchase some opal to depart with, and thus a great demand for choice opal is created.

If one travels around the world and takes time to observe and visit the jewelry stores in other lands, he will find that outstanding gem opal is poorly represented. He will observe a window full of diamonds, rubies, emeralds, and sapphires, but only a lone opal or two will be displayed. This situation exists through no fault of the jeweler. He is in business to sell gems—any gems—and while opal is in demand the world over, the stones he desires are difficult to obtain. Opal, in most countries of the world, is advertised by the jewelry trade as the birthstone for the month of April. In my home city of San Francisco, where we have hundreds of jewelry stores, I made it a point of interest to undertake a personal canvas and to visit many of these establishments. I can, without fear of contradiction, state that there are probably no more than twenty, perhaps twenty-five, outstanding opal gems that could be classified as tops. Outside of two stores in our Chinatown which feature quite an excellent assortment of opals—some mounted and others unmounted

—of very fine quality, there are only a few others that possess noteworthy ones. One store had a very fine mounted cabochon of about 12 carats priced at $1,500; several others had a few on display that ranged in price from $250 to $500.

In all cities outside of those in Australia, one will find a similar situation. As I have noted above, this is through no fault of the jeweler. He naturally desires opal. In most cases, he wants top-quality gems, but he can obtain only the cheaper quality, for which his customers will pay only so much.

So, in answer to the question "Is opal scarce?" I would say that truly outstanding gems are indeed scarce. The world traveler will view thousands of other gems on display for every distinguished opal that he finds. Many stores do feature the cheaper and poorer grades, and there is no disgrace in investing in these if the purchaser cannot afford the higher-priced gems. Some jewelers, when they are asked for opals and either have none or have a very limited stock, will, as a business ruse, have an excuse. This will usually be to claim that the reason he has no opal is that opal is not a popular gem or that it is not much in demand. Of course this is far from the truth.

I have dealt in opal for over thirty-five years and am one of the original organizers of the San Francisco Gem and Mineral Society and of the East Bay Gem and Mineral Society, situated in Oakland, California. These are now two outstanding societies and are comprised of a great many members (the San Francisco society has over 600) among whom only a very few who have specialized in and collected the gem have any idea of just what value it commands. This lack of knowledge is, of course, not restricted to these fine groups. It extends to the general public. Naturally it must be understood that a great many members of all gem and mineral societies have a restricted income and therefore find it impossible to obtain the more expensive varieties. Still, this does not excuse them for not having a better understanding of the values of the gem.

Perhaps another factor is that over the years a great many so-called dealers in gems and minerals have unscrupulously advertised "outstanding" opal at ridiculously low prices. Of course the material offered was, as a rule, of the cheap, white milk variety, at from $2 to $5 per ounce, and some have even advertised choice opal by the pound. Such opal must by any reasoning be plain rubbish and incapable of producing gems.

Unfortunately, there is no law that governs so-called dealers in opal, and in practically all cases these "dealers" know little or nothing of the gem. One would think that with our present-day education extending to so many areas and with hundreds of gem and mineral societies existing all over the nation, even amateur lapidaries and collectors would have a greater understanding of the material and be able to distinguish the difference between the high-priced gem material and plain rubbish—in some cases little better than potch.

I have many times advised amateur lapidaries who have mainly wanted outstanding rough-opal gem material at a very low price. It was necessary for me to advise them that prices of opal are no different from those of other desirable gem materials. I have had to ask these folks what they would expect if they were offered a diamond at $5 a carat. And of course they never even thought that they might obtain a piece of glass at that price. So it is with opal.

Opal at its source is the same as diamonds at their source in Johannesburg, South Africa. When the opal is mined—even before the buyers obtain it—it is valued by a valuator residing in the field. Even the smallest pieces are studiously examined, and every last piece is snipped to ascertain its interior colors and beauty. This is done by the valuator, who receives a fee from the miner, who, it must be understood, not being a cutter, has a very limited idea of a finished gem or its price. He is simply the miner. So anyone who imagines that he is going to obtain a remarkable gem among those in the cheap, poorer grades—something the valuator in the field has perhaps overlooked—has another thought coming.

The only advice I can offer to those who wish to purchase opal either in its rough state or as finished gems is that they should first correspond with some reliable opal dealer in Australia. With present-day air-mail service, this can be done in a matter of a few days. If the prospective purchaser does not know of any such dealers, he can obtain the necessary information by writing to the Australian Trade Commissioner, Washington, D.C., or the Australian Consul, San Francisco, California, or the Australian Ambassador, Washington, D.C. All of these will be glad to be of service.

One may ask what has become of all the grand opals of great value. Some of these can be seen in museums, such as the Smithsonian Institution (the National Museum) in Washington, D.C.; the Museum of Natural History in New York City; the Field Museum in Chicago; the British Museum in London; and of course the numerous Australian museums, to mention only a few.

It was during the reign of Queen Victoria that the gem world was first introduced to the Australian opal, and the queen was presented with some of the finest of the period. Queen Alexandra also possessed some splendid gems, and England's present ruler, Queen Elizabeth, was presented with a magnificent opal when she toured Australia a few years ago. Unlike those of the former queens, which all came from Lightning Ridge, Queen Elizabeth's opal came from the Andamooka field.

The famous gem known as the Southern Cross was purchased by the former khedive of Egypt. Emperor Menelik of Ethiopia was an ardent admirer of opal and purchased many stones. Kaiser Wilhelm of Germany ordered his ambassador to Australia to obtain opals for him. These are only a few of the notables who became possessors of valuable opals.

As in the case of outstanding diamonds, a great many fine opals have been known by name. Two of these are the Empress Eugénie and the Butterfly. The King Midas was obtained by Czar Nicholas II of Russia and no doubt is now on exhibit at the museum in Leningrad. Practically all the nabobs and maharajahs of India obtained the best opals procurable. The Star of Australia was purchased by a collector from Los Angeles from Percy Marks of Sydney. The Bird of Paradise was obtained by the late J. Pierpont Morgan for the Morgan collection. He was an ardent collector not only of opal but of all gem stones and once delegated a gem dealer to make a special trip to Australia for opals. (I was personally acquainted with this gem dealer, who had an open checkbook.) Lily Langtry was presented by an admirer with a prize stone known as the Gem Orchid. This stone, it was said, cost 2,000 pounds or close to $10,000 according to the rate of exchange prevailing at that time.

The wealthy Chinese sought opal, along with jade and tourmaline, these being the only gem stones the Chinese people really admire. Of course there are a great many fine and costly opals in private collections. One distinguished collection of opals is owned by Mr. Harmon Blethen of Oakland, California—a collection that he often exhibits at mineral and gem society conventions held in the West.

13 Superstitions Regarding Opals

ARE OPALS unlucky? There are many people in all parts of the world who are easily induced to believe in superstitions. I once laughingly asked a famous gemmologist if opal was unlucky. He said: "It certainly is. It is very unlucky if you are unfortunate enough not to have any." This is just about the best answer I have encountered.

Many years ago, a considerable number of ignorant people were imbued with the idea that opals were unlucky. None, of course, ever asked why. But this rumor at one time did have wide publicity. It was originated and circulated by a combine of crooks who were purchasing opal at the Lightning Ridge field during the period of its greatest productivity. They found considerable competition from the other buyers, mainly those from the capitals of Europe. So, in order to offset these buyers and to discredit opal, thereby getting rid of the competition and gaining control of the buying, they circulated the rumor that opal was unlucky. However, their efforts were unrewarded, for the rumor never stopped the other buyers; neither did it affect to any extent the demand for the gem. In all probability, those who told their friends that they did not wish to have the gem because it was unlucky did not have the funds to obtain it and thereby displayed a case of sour grapes.

The circulators of this superstitious rumor were somewhat aided at the time by an incident that occurred at Queen Victoria's coronation. The queen had been presented with a large and beautiful opal from Lightning Ridge, and this opal was mounted in a pin or brooch that was used to fasten her gown or her train at the back. When the procession was moving down the aisle in Westminster Abbey, this pin came loose, and some adjustments were in order. This little incident gave the rumormongers additional ammunition for propaganda. They said: "We told you so. Told you opal was unlucky." However, all this "unlucky" propaganda has now been forgotten and has died out completely.

I had considerable amusement at one time in regard to this superstition. So did all my friends and acquaintances when I showed them a letter I had received from a chap. This fellow had written asking for some rough opal, which was duly sent to him. After a couple of weeks, back came the opal, accompanied by this letter of great wailing and sadness. The letter stated that since he had received the opal his wife had run off with a lover, he had lost a very fine prospective buyer for his home, his dog had run away, and his taxes had been raised. The letter also stated that he had had nothing but bad luck ever since he had received this opal and that even if there were no refund, he was glad to get rid of it. Naturally I refunded the poor man his money, writing him a letter in the same vein, admitting that things could not possibly get worse, and trusting that his luck would soon change for the better.

When it comes to a discussion of lucky men in the trade, no work on opal would be complete without some mention of the late Harry Brukarz, who was in a way just as noteworthy a character as many of the men of a past era about whom much has been written. Harry Brukarz owned and operated the opal and curio shop on the corner of Castlereagh Street and Martin Place in the Hotel Australia building in Sydney. He was known to thousands of people not only in Australia but throughout the entire world. No visitor or tourist could have failed to see and usually visit his excellent establishment. Members of ship and airplane crews were also fascinated by the opal he always had on display. Although he dealt in other lines too, opals were his first love. Many miners brought their opals to him for sale, and he always paid them honest prices. Therefore he was always well supplied. He was always one of the first persons I visited on arrival in Australia, and I always received a grand welcome.

Harry usually knew that I would be walking down Martin Place about 3 P.M. At that time of day he would be standing outside his store leaning against an iron railing. On my approach he would take my arm, saying: "You're just the man I want to see." Then he would lead me into the back room of the store, where one of his beautiful salesgirls would usually be serving tea. Any visitor would have to partake of afternoon tea. While we were sipping our tea, Harry would reach down and produce a sack of opals. Of course he loved to bargain. One particular time I well recall. He was displaying a sack containing probably 15 or 20 ounces of very good quality opal and asking a reasonable price for it. Since I was to be in town the following morning, I decided to pass up an immediate purchase. The opal, however, being of nice quality, I wanted it. Next morning I arrived and was welcomed as usual. I asked: "Harry, where is that sack of opal we were looking at yesterday afternoon?"

"Oh, that lot," he said. "Two Japanese gentlemen arrived after you left and took the lot."

Thus I found out that when you are buying opal in the rough, you make up your mind and don't waste time playing around. It's a case of take it now or leave it. Don't come back looking for it.

Harry Brukarz was known to every Australian, regardless of whether he resided in a city or in the outback in the bush. Not even Sir. Robert Gordon Menzies, the prime minister, was better known. For Harry was known as the Lottery King. He had more luck in winning the lotteries than any man who ever lived. He won the New South Wales government lottery first prize of 12,000 pounds ($27,000) several times, as well as countless second and third prizes. All the citizens of Sydney wanted to know his system, but if there ever was any system, the secret died with him.

Always, when I visited him, he would invite me to share a couple of lottery tickets with him. Arriving at his store one day, I was greeted with the news: "We have won 500 pounds ($1,125)." There wasn't a man in Australia who wouldn't have shared a lottery ticket with him. At one time he won 50 pounds (about $112) but did not go to collect it. When I asked him why, he said it was not worth bothering with. Whether or not he ever collected it I never knew. Many magazines and newspapers wrote of his phenomenal luck. Some even went so far as to suggest that he must have had the drawings fixed. This, of course, would have been impossible, since the drawings are open to the public.

Everyone who ever met or dealt with Harry Brukarz liked the man. He never married, and his relatives carry on where he left off. With his recent passing, his thousands of friends lost a man who loved his opals. And yet the world abounds with those who, in ignorance, still insist that opals are unlucky!

14 The Preservation of Opals

MANY PEOPLE have observed opal placed in bottles of some fluid or other. A great many of the beautiful pieces from the Rainbow Ridge mine in Nevada are seen in this manner. The fluid is usually glycerine or clear mineral oil; sometimes water is used. The idea is that the fluid has a tendency to prevent the opal from cracking. In this respect it does help to some extent. It also has the effect of greatly increasing its beauty by magnification, but if the opal is taken out of the solution and exposed to the atmosphere, in time it will crack. A great many people have thought that through this method the opal would in due time be "cured" —that is, cured of its spider-web cracking tendency. They are entirely misled.

For years, scientists, mineralogists, and others have tried various means of curing the opal of cracking. Some have buried it in damp clay for long periods of time or have placed it in water. I know of one person who placed an opal from Nevada in a damp mortar for a few years, but when it was released it still continued to craze. At one time I was offered a large percentage of the output of the Rainbow Ridge mine in Nevada if I would disclose the method used in Australia to make the opal durable and eliminate its tendency to crack—this in order that gem stones could be cut from it. Of course I had to advise that so far this had been found impossible, that the opal from Australian fields did not crack on exposure, and that miners and others used no method to ensure its durability in order to cut it.

Dr. Dake, noted authority and editor of the *Mineralogist*,

who has visited Rainbow Ridge on many occasions and has studied this opal and its characteristics, states that if opal from there did cut into a cabochon it would certainly check later. The checking will usually take place within a matter of a few years or even less. In rare cases it may be delayed for years. Dr. Dake informs me that he has an opal pendant from this field weighing 35 carats. This was the first opal "cured" and then carefully cut by an expert. It survived for fifteen years without checking, but eventually checking appeared.

Dr. Dake states that this checking is perhaps due to dehydration or internal stress and says that the latter is most probable. I should assume also that temperature change could play a part in this phenomenon. The checks usually appear on the surface of the cabochon, involving only a thin depth. In some cases the checks have been ground away and the cabochon has been refinished, of course with the hope that the stone will remain intact. Dr. Dake further states: "We have never had any reliable information in which this hope has proven true." I may add that it is very doubtful that it would ever prove true.

Dr. Dake goes on to say that "it would appear that every Rainbow Ridge opal, cut or uncut, will eventually undergo this physical change of checking. In the case of a cut stone, it would appear that, given time, checking is most certain to appear. A large rough mass may require some years. Storing the cabochon in water, glycerine, or oil is no assurance that checking will be avoided." In the case of the opal pendant that Dr. Dake referred to, this stone was kept in glycerine 99 percent of the fifteen years, and it was taken out at intervals to be worn for only a few hours as a necklace.

15 Equipment for Gem Production

THE EQUIPMENT used for the production of gem opal from the mined rough material is not too elaborate; neither is it expensive. In fact, the assembly can be rather toylike, small, and compact.

First in order, of course, is the saw. Since very little rough opal is larger than 2 inches by 1 inch in size, a small gem saw, of which many are illustrated and advertised in the various lapidary and mineral journals, will do. This small machine should accommodate a bronze or copper diamond blade of 5-inch diameter and a thickness no greater than .012 inch. Such a blade saves much valuable material, especially if it is of carat value.

Next in order is the grinding wheel, which is used for the shaping of the piece cut by the saw. Since opal grinds to shape very easily, a wheel of 8-inch diameter, 1-inch thickness, and 320 grit is sufficient, and only one wheel is needed.

The next implement is the sander. A sander of 8-inch diameter, 3 inches in width, and 320 grit is ideal for the sanding operation.

For the final operation of polishing, an 8-inch disc with either leather or felt covering will suffice. Tin oxide (stannic acid) is the polishing agent and is applied wet with a small brush to produce a mirror finish.

I use a combination assembly of grinder, sander, and polishing disc, all assembled on one shaft supplied with pans and splash covers purchased from the Highland Park Lapidary Equipment Company, Pasadena, California. This gives ideal service and takes up very little space. Similar assem-

Plate 33: Compact gem saw. It is small but efficient and uses a 5-inch diamond-charged blade rotating at 3,000 r.p.m. Water coolant in pit.

Plate 34: Grinding wheel with sander and polishing wheel on end. Water coolant on the 8-inch grinder.

Plate 35: 12-inch cast-iron lap rotating at 300 r.p.m. Used for bevels and flats, it is operated with a 320-grit abrasive.

Plate 36: 8-inch polishing disc has leather face, backed with rubber or felt padding. Tin oxide is used as the polishing agent.

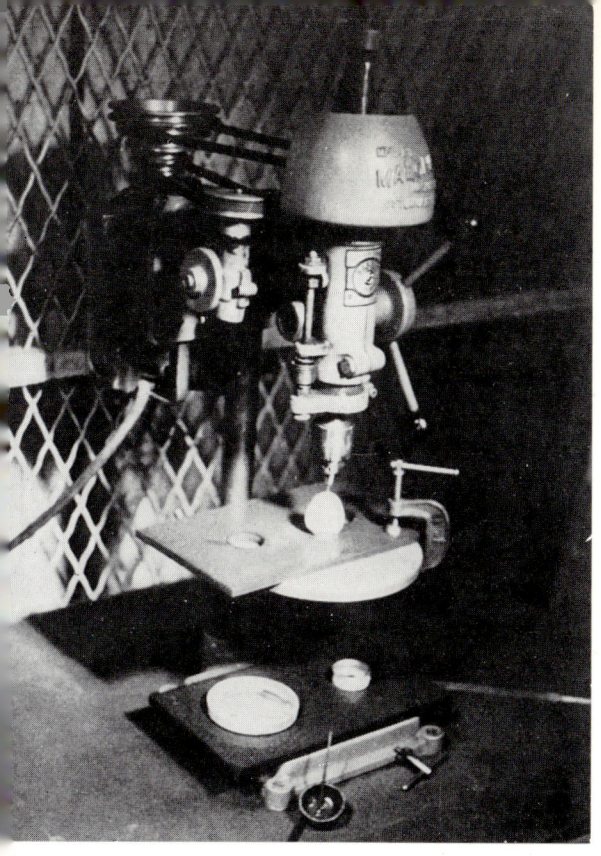

Plate 37: Small but efficient light-duty drill-press for manual or automatic operation, with regulated pressure. It uses either a small core or a diamond drill.

Plate 38: Assorted tools used in gem production. Dop sticks, loupe, lamps, sealing wax, knife, tweezers, and alcohol.

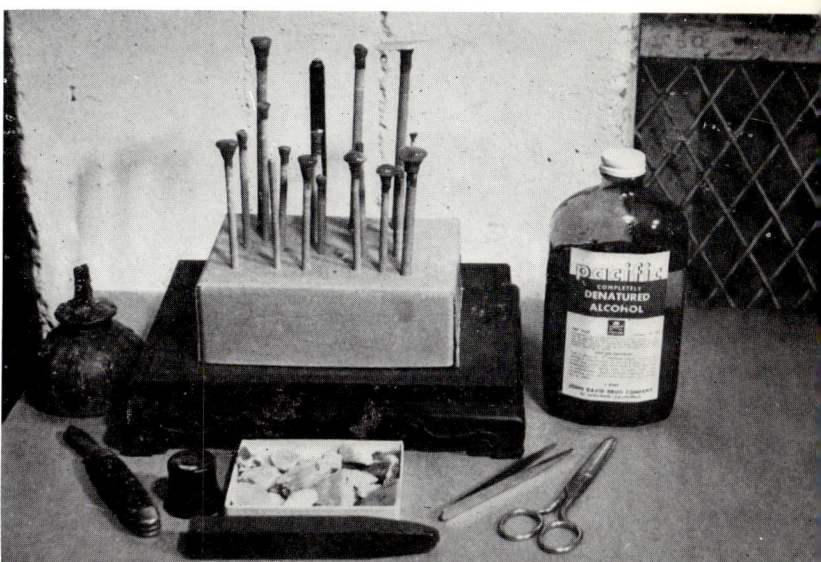

Plate 39: High-speed hand tool with saws, bits, and grinders Used for various carving operations in opal production.

blies are advertised by other companies in the lapidary, gem, and mineral magazines.

A lap wheel of 8- or 10-inch diameter is a very handy item to have, but it is not essential. However, it does have its uses, especially when the cutter wishes to lap flat surfaces or to bevel a stone. The lap can be of any metal, cast iron being most commonly used. It is operated by applying silicon carbide (carborundum) of 320 grit for the abrasive agent. Even a lucite lap will work with efficiency.

If one wishes to produce pendants and to eliminate bell-cap mountings, a small light-duty drill is desirable. Opal is very easily drilled, and the use of small tube drills or diamond drills of 1- to 1.5-mm. diameter is recommended. These can be purchased from dealers advertising lapidary equipment. Drilling should be accomplished with very light pressure on the drill, applying 320-grit carborundum or norbide as the drilling agent for tube drills.

Other items of equipment, easily obtained, are noted in the following rundown of the complete assembly: saw, grinding wheel, sander, polishing wheel, lap wheel, 320-grit carborundum for the lap, tin oxide for polishing, small drill press with assorted tube drills, magnifying loupe, alcohol lamp (made from a lubricating-oil can), dop sticks cut from dowels, an ounce of norbide abrasive for the drilling agent, sealing wax for the cementing of stones on dop sticks, and a plastic apron for protecting clothing from splash.

16 The Cutting of the Gem

THE CUTTING and polishing of the gem from the rough material is a very enlightening and fascinating procedure. At the same time it is a simple operation, for the gem offers no difficult problems, even to the amateur. When a piece of rough opal is to be fashioned, the operator should first study the subject in great detail. If this is done, good results can be obtained, even from the cheaper grades. Much white milk opal, for instance, is veined with very attractive color bands. If these are viewed not from the top but from the sides, the operator should either saw or lap the piece down to this band of color, being very careful not to overdo the operation. Care must be taken so that this color vein is not lost by lapping, sawing, or other procedures.

After this procedure has produced a color plane from the vein, the next step is to inspect the specimen and see what it will possibly produce. If the piece is irregular in shape, for instance, the retaining of its size is important. Here the operator will have to use some artistic taste to determine what size and shape he will finally choose. Size and shape are two distinct factors. Perhaps the stone can be a regular cabochon or an oblong; perhaps it will be better to produce a square. This is what the operator now has to decide. Of course, in the case of an expensive and high-quality gem it is important to fashion it in such a way that the greatest size possible is produced. This is understandable, since precious opal is bought and sold by the carat only.

A great many pieces of rough opal are not so large that the use of a saw is always necessary, but where material is large enough it is desirable to include a small gem saw in the equipment. Such a machine is not expensive. I use a very small machine 12 by 8 by 6 inches. It is supplied with a miniature vise, although I hold the material to be sawed in my hand. The rough opal being small as a rule, precision work can be done in this way, the sawing of any piece taking only a few minutes, more or less. Many manufacturers of lapidary equipment sell gem saw machines equipped with 8-inch-diameter blades of .035-inch thickness. Such saws, however, are not desirable for opal or valuable gem cutting, since a heavy blade of this type will waste the material. The saw that I use is fitted with a 5-inch-diameter blade of .012-inch thickness. I eliminate the lap because fine professional results can be obtained here without it, but if a small blade of 8-inch diameter is desired, it can at times come in handy for lapping flat pieces, using only a very fine abrasive no coarser than 320 grit.

After the desired section has been produced, the next operation is the grinding of the specimen to the distinct shape. This should be done by hand on an abrasive grinding wheel of 8-inch diameter and 320 grit. Only this grinding wheel is necessary. There is absolutely no need of two grinders and certainly none of coarser grit. Opal, being a delicate gem, grinds fast enough on this one wheel.

It is important that the face of the grinding wheel always be kept flat and free of bumps and grooves. In order to accomplish this, one should have a half-carat-diamond wheel dresser. This is a very inexpensive tool that will keep the face of the grinding wheel in a true condition. Place a straight flat board on the splash pan at the center of the grinder, allow the water to run on it, start the diamond wheel dresser gently at the edge of the grinder, and roll the shank of the dresser along the board. After repeating this operation several times across the face of the grinder, you will have it smooth and true, so that bevels and edging can easily be placed on flat faces and square stones can be shaped with the utmost precision.

The operator shaping his opal on the grinder should be advised that according to professional standards the bottom or underside of the stone should, wherever possible, be rounded; even stones finished with a flat face should have a rounded bottom. Two-piece opals or doublets should also be finished this way. It would be advisable for the beginner or the amateur to inspect some unmounted gems, or even stones in open mountings, so as to become more fully acquainted with this particular pattern. It will be found that jade is also fashioned in this manner. Agates and many other stones are usually shaped with a flat bottom. I have never been able to ascertain the reason for the cutting of opals in this shape, but I suspect that opal in a great many fine pieces in the rough has a very unorthodox shape because of sloping and uneven edges, and this particular shape will tend to save the size and weight better than a flat-bottomed shape will.

Grind and shape the bottom of the gem first. If for any reason difficulty is experienced in shaping by hand, it will be found that it is easier to grind with the gem cemented on a dop stick. To place the stone on the dop stick, I use dowels (in Australia, butcher's skewers). These can be purchased at any lumber or building-supply house. The gem should be slightly heated, either by holding it with tweezers over an alcohol flame or by placing it upon a heater, being extremely careful not to overheat it. Any gem stone, even agate, will tend to crack if overheated. Opal is no different. In fact, having a slight water content, opal will more readily do so. If the stone is only slightly warm, the melted sealing wax on the end of the dop stick will adhere to it. The dop stick should be held up and the stone viewed to be sure it is level. After the gem has been satisfactorily dopped, it is ground, and after this comes the sanding.

This is a very important feature. I use an 8-inch by 3-inch wheel with a 320-grit cloth, backed with either felt or sponge rubber. The reason for this operation is to sand off any high spots left by the grinding wheel and also to eliminate all scratches. When this cloth is first used, it will tend to cut very fast, so care should be taken to use light pressure only. With a used cloth, extra pressure can be applied. Care should also be taken at intervals by feeling the stone to make sure it does not become overheated. This operation is very easy and simple and will give considerable satisfaction if one employs the movement across the face of the sander with inspection from time to time for the elimination of all bumps and scratches. The result will be a semipolish. After sanding, wash the gem—still on the dop stick—so as to be sure that no grit from the sander adheres to it.

Next we turn to the polishing wheel. I use an 8-inch aluminum disc covered with a light oil-free leather and backed by either heavy felt or sponge rubber. Tin oxide mixed with water and applied with a small brush is used as the polishing agent. If the gem has been properly sanded, this final polishing operation is very rapid. Just a few minutes will produce a mirror finish on the gem. Now the gem can be removed from the dop stick by holding it down on a cloth and separating it with a sharp knife. Any sealing wax adhering to it can readily be removed by dipping the stone in alcohol for a few minutes. The gem is now finished and ready for the mounting.

17 The Doublet or Two-Piece Opal

JUST WHAT is a doublet? It is a very thin section of precious opal cemented upon a base of potch, another term for common opal. As pointed out in another chapter, eighty percent of all opal jewelry is doublet or two-piece opal. If one could observe opal as it is mined, especially at the Australian fields, he would note that a great amount of it is no more than an eighth of an inch in thickness. Usually these veins are of the very finest quality. Lapidaries discovered that by lapping off the dirt or matrix on each side beautiful opal could be produced. But such a thin section would not suffice to shape a stone in the usual manner.

Even a thin section only an eighth of an inch in thickness is sometimes too thick for a doublet. I observed in my visits to Australian lapidary establishments that this opal is valued and that therefore none of it is wasted. Sometimes a very thin piece is even sawed in half. I found that the Australian lapidaries were very efficient—much more so and much more advanced than lapidaries in the United States or Europe—when it came to the working of opal. Since it is a home product, well they should be. I believe that if I were shown a doublet anywhere in the world, I could tell whether it was fashioned in Australia or elsewhere. I have at various times pointed out to American lapidaries the characteristics that constitute this difference. I have asked them if they could duplicate the work. Usually they would be observing it for the first time and could only state that they would try to do so.

My purpose in the present chapter is to discuss how doublets are made and to point out what their distinguishing characteristics are. The method of making doublets is not complicated, but skill and precision are of utmost importance.

First a thin section of opal is made either by sawing or lapping. (It is lapped down as thin as one, two, or three millimeters—rarely any thicker.) A section sawed or lapped to that dimension is almost transparent if held up to the light. It will usually show no semblance of color. But when the section is laid upon a black background, wet, it will then display the beautiful colors of which it is capable. This is really very remarkable for such a thin section—one which, I have often observed, is in some cases so light that it will float on water. Here I may mention that no opal in the world from any of the other localities will successfully make a doublet in this manner. If such opals are backed with black in this way, they will not be enhanced by the procedure. The Australian opal alone produces this peculiar phenomenon.

After the given thin section has been cut and lapped to the desired thickness, a piece of potch (common opal) is fashioned for the base section with a flat surface for the top and a rounded one for the bottom. This base section in Australia is always potch opal. The most desirable is a dark slate-colored variety found extensively at the Lightning Ridge field. This material is always bought by the local cutters, and a good price is paid for it. Some American lapidaries substitute black onyx or black obsidian for the base. I asked Australian opal cutters why they did not use these materials for the base. They stated that they had to have opal on opal; otherwise it would not be a two-piece opal but a half-and-half. So they strictly adhere to this principle, and no jewelry store would think of purchasing a cutter's output if it were made otherwise. So the Australian doublet is always a true two-piece opal.

Once the base has been fashioned, a mixture of flake shellac suitably colored with black carbon (lamp black) is heated over an alcohol lamp, and a thin coat of this is applied to each side to be set. Both the opal section and the base are slightly heated. Then the thin opal section is placed in position on the base, and some pressure is applied in order to exclude any air bubbles.

Next the opal top is further shaped to fit the base by use of a grinding wheel or sander with a fine 320-grit carborundum cloth and is then polished on a wet felt or leather wheel, with tin oxide as the polishing agent. During any of the operations only a light touch or pressure can be used, and care must be taken that no extreme heat is generated. In that case the opal will move, and too much heat transmitted to the work will result in a fracture of the opal.

Now if one inspects the finished two-piece opal cut in Australia, he will observe that the cutter has placed a sharp and distinct bezel all around the base section. This is done, of course, so that the crimping of the mounting will not crush the thin opal. Other lapidaries know this, and they also make allowance for the mounting; but instead of a sharp and distinct bezel they usually only slope the edge of the opal where it joins the base.

In my recent experiments with the fashioning of doublets, I have arrived at a very much easier and simpler means of cementing the gem-opal slice to the base material. The process described above—the application of flake shellac as the cementing agent—has been the method used by all professional lapidaries up to the present time. This method entails a very tedious and exacting procedure. Flake shellac is generally not very easy to obtain; the heating of the shellac and the opal sometimes causes the opal to fracture; and air bubble elimination is also a problem. My new discovery has come about through the recent perfection of an adhesive now nationally advertised as Epoxy. This is used with a catalyst called a hardener. The set is sold today in most hardware stores as a unit. Two types of Epoxy are manufactured: one white, the other clear. For our purpose the clear type is desirable.

Take a small amount of the Epoxy, mix with a tooth pick enough lamp black to color, apply very sparingly and evenly to both the base potch and the gem slice, press together, allow to harden (usually overnight is sufficient). With the use of this new cement no air bubbles will result, and no heat is necessary. The cementing is extremely durable, for, if for any reason one attempts to remove the opal, it will be found that the cement is just as hard as the subject and impossible to remove without breaking it. So one need have no fears of the opal's coming loose for any reason whatever.

18 Some Opal Peculiarities

IT HAS been observed that where color planes or lines exist, especially in white opal, these lines are always parallel. They are never on a vertical plane. Just why this color should always be parallel in the built-up gelatinous mass is a mystery. Yet in the expensive gem types the colors are distributed throughout the entire area.

Anyone who has photographed opal on color film has found that the result never does justice to the colors. When a photographer, for instance, photographs an orchid or a rose, his photos will show the flowers almost true and perfect in relation to the actual colors and also extremely natural in appearance. He cannot obtain such results with opal. Similarly, opal viewed under fluorescent lighting will not be observed to best advantage. But if it is viewed by ordinary electric light, outdoor light, or even candlelight, the opal will come to life in all its glory.

Another interesting observation that I have made over many years is that no jeweler or lapidary anywhere can duplicate a precious opal. It stands alone. He can readily duplicate the diamond or any other gem, but not the opal. This does not refer to the cheaper white types of opal with, for instance, pin-fire colors. A duplication can to some extent be obtained from the rough of this.

Some years ago a distinguished lady customer in Washington, D.C., sent me her opal ring, which she had accidentally broken. She wanted a duplication. I inspected at least several hundred stones and failed to find one that reasonably matched hers. I then took the problem to my good friend Francis S. Sperisen, author of *The Art of the Lapidary* and an outstanding and accomplished commercial lapidary with a large stock of stones for the trade. He looked over his stock and failed to produce a stone to match. We had to settle on another fine gem, and we sent it on with an explanation to the lady, who understood the problem.

Another thing not universally known is that no opal from any other source but Australia will produce a doublet or (in Australian terminology) a two-piece opal for commercial use. The opal from Querétaro, for instance, is fashioned like the Australian doublet, but the effect of its color is not enhanced. Australian jelly-type opals, when cut and polished and then placed upon a black background, will show to greater advantage; their appearance will change entirely. But jelly opal from any other source will not be changed in appearance by this method.

Dendritic inclusions in opal are the same as those often observed in some varieties of agate. They usually resemble branching treelike figures and ferns. These inclusions are crystallized forms of the mineral manganese. They are to be observed only in the massive common opal deposits and are never found in the precious gem opal.

Certain terms used in relation to opal are worth mentioning. Opaline has the meaning of "like opal" and is used to describe such things as opalescent glass. Girasol is sometimes used to refer to opal giving out firelike reflections in bright light. It is also at times called fire opal. Recently advertisements have appeared in some journals describing an item called agate opalized. Of course no such thing is possible. Such an item is either agate or opal. Opalite is not a recognized mineral word but is sometimes used in reference to common opal.

The word "pseudomorph" means false form: something with an irregular or deceptive form. In mineralogy it is a mineral having the characteristic outward form of another species. In regard to opal, we speak of opal pseudomorph after wood or a clam or whatever the case may be. Wollaston reportedly suggested that a certain authority claimed the Lightning Ridge opal to be a pseudomorph after coral. He did not disclose who this authority might have been. But I cannot believe that Wollaston, being the eminent mineralogist he was, thought this to be the case. I have seen hundreds of Lightning Ridge opals in their rough state but have never noted a single indication that the opal there is a pseudomorph after coral or anything else.

There have been many pseudomorphs in the occurrence of opal. The White Cliffs field in New South Wales was noted especially for opal replacement of clams. These were in many instances solid gem material of the very highest quality. Some opal replacements, however, are not of gem quality. Opal replacements or pseudomorphs of oysters, snails, mussels, and other mollusks, and even of fish vertebrae and wood and limb sections have been found. At the Virgin Valley location in Nevada a great deal of opal replacement of wood and also swamp flora is in evidence, but I have never observed any of the marine mollusk varieties like those of the Australian fields. The opal at Querétaro in Mexico produces no pseudomorphs; the entire region being igneous and the opal being found in rhyolite, such occurrences as replacements of mollusks would not be possible.

Opal has always had such an attraction for some miners that they absolutely refuse to sell or part with certain pieces, regardless of the price offered and even when they may be devoid of funds. In most camps and tents, candles are used for light, and it is not unusual for a miner to get up in the night, light his candle, produce his opal, and marvel at its beauty. He is entranced by it. One would be amazed to observe how the light of a single candle will bring out a display of spectacular grandeur. In fact, the display of remarkable colors will be even more magnificent than by sunlight or electric light.

19 On to Lightning Ridge

HAVING attended school in Australia, I gained a very reasonable education in regard to the geology and the geography as well as, in later years, the mineral resources of the land. Understanding the customs of the people was also an asset, especially when one traveled to what Australians call the outback. In earlier times one did not have to travel very far from the large cities before he found himself in the outback. Having known and read much about the great opal fields and of Lightning Ridge in particular, I decided it was a must to go forth and see for myself.

Located in Sydney, which is a modern city of approximately two million people (about the same size and population as Los Angeles today), I made it my first task to inquire how to get to the Ridge, as it is called by the locals living there. Wherever I went and whomever I spoke to, I met with the same results. Few had even heard of the place, and none had any idea of how to get there. I was even given a blank stare at the large central railroad station. The gentleman who handled the information and inquiries had no idea where it was, and he gave me a dark look, no doubt for asking a silly question, which all information men are of course subject to. Of course, since Lightning Ridge is not on any railroad, I had to forgive him for his lack of knowledge.

At last my salvation lay in a railway map of the state of New South Wales. Lightning Ridge was marked on this map, but its population was not stated. The map showed that the northwestern railroad line terminated at Walgett, about 450 miles northwest of Sydney. Lightning Ridge was still about 50 miles to the north of Walgett. Another thing to be considered was this : when one did arrive at the Ridge, were there any accommodations? Could one obtain anything to eat? No one knew a thing. These matters are something that one has to prepare for in the great outback of Australia. Like many others in the past, I had read that the place was desert, that it was also a ghost town, and that it was not a very enticing place for one to be traveling to with nothing more than a suitcase containing some working clothes and snakebite medicine and with no advice whatever as to what to expect. So, carrying my trusty maps, I bought a ticket to Walgett and departed at 2 P.M. on the Western Mail.

I was very fortunate in having a fine companion in my compartment, a nurse going home to Walgett on her vacation. She had no idea how I was to get to the Ridge after arriving at Walgett. She explained the country we passed through, which was mainly wide open spaces with some areas where grass was growing like wheat among the small trees. We came to small towns about every fifty miles or so. One saw no roads, no houses or humans after leaving the towns. The engineer every so often would blow the whistle, looking out the window. Large herds of kangaroo would be seen jumping off in their haste. Again the whistle would sound, and this time there would be a large flock of emus scampering for safety. The nurse took no notice of all this and was highly amused at my interest; to her it seemed an everyday occurrence.

We arrived next afternoon at Walgett, the end of the railroad line. One rather odd fact that I never could explain is that in almost all Australian country towns I have visited the railroad station is placed as much as a mile out of town. Walgett was no exception. The only thing I could ever make of it was that one just had to patronize the taxicab man, which of course everyone does. The taxi soon delivered us to the local hotel. Walgett boasts of one only; thus, if you arrive without reservation, you are indeed fortunate if you can obtain a room. Here at last we were in Walgett, a small place about two blocks long, very similar to some of our small towns in Nevada or Arizona.

Now, how do you get to the Ridge? Everyone knew all about the place and where it was, but no one knew how you got there. After many inquiries I at last met a very helpful chap. Said he: "Go to the post office and ask the man what time the truck leaves with the mail and freight for the Ridge." Mind you, a truck. No bus here. At the post office the man said it left at 9:30 in the morning. Said I: "Better look up the driver and make arrangements." However, no one knew who or where the driver was or where to locate him. Naturally I was up early next morning so as to contact that truck driver. As the post office was only a block away, it was no problem for me to keep any truck in sight.

I may mention that Walgett is an extremely wealthy wool-shipping center. Some of the world's finest merino wool is produced within the few hundred square miles around it. Taking a walk after breakfast to the post office to watch for trucks, I was amazed to observe at least thirty dogs of all colors and sizes resting up out on the red dusty road. One large chap, the largest greyhound I ever saw, made friends, and he accompanied me on my walk. An approaching man smiled; so I asked: "Who owns him?" He said: "No one does." I then asked what all of the other dogs were doing lying out on the road. He stated that they were all waiting for breakfast, adding that the highway engineer was now having his breakfast in the hotel, and when he came out, he would go to the butcher's shop and load up a wheelbarrow he owned and would then wheel the full barrow to the highway department. And all the dogs would eat. I will say, all those dogs did look as though they received foreign

Plate 40: The Kite brothers at their temporary camp on the Nine Mile, Lightning Ridge.

Plate 41: The Kite brothers' claim at the Nine Mile. From the right: Shirl, Luke, and Bill Kite.

aid, for they were all peaceful, contented, and in the best of condition.

At last a truck drove up to the post office. I asked the young chap driving it if he was going to Lightning Ridge. "That's right," he said. He was leaving as soon as he'd loaded the mail. The truck was already stacked high with miscellaneous freight. He stated that he would be glad to have me ride with him. En route he would stop often, and I helped him unload freight for some sheep station that was represented only by a large mailbox with the name on it. The homestead might be as far away as ten miles, but they knew the time and days the truck went through on its way north and up into the state of Queensland.

Arriving at Lightning Ridge, I was surprised to observe that the place was neither a ghost town nor a desert. For a mile or so along the approach to the ridge itself, we passed through thousands of dumps which were all white and could be seen in every direction. They had the look of huge ant hills. The grass was green, and small stunted trees grew in abundance. Later on, after I had described to a native citizen my surprise at the nice prosperous surroundings, he said: "Yes, this year we have had good rains. See this dusty dirt road? Well, in droughts the whole country looks like this road—not a single blade of grass anywhere. In those periods hundreds of thousands of sheep starve or die of thirst."

I found a very nice and comfortable country-style hotel of about a dozen rooms, the Imperial by name, and soon was acquainted with the licensee, a Mr. Jim Duncan, and his good wife, who between them operated the entire place. A visitor from the United States was somewhat of a curiosity. There was one other guest, a lady who stated she was obtaining the history of the place and experiences for a book. For some unknown reason, the locals did not look upon her with favor or, for that matter, upon me either, till they were assured that I was not some spy for the tax collector. I was appointed to a room which had recently been vacated by the bishop. This was amusing to the local boys, who said that the bishop had passed through to give any of the locals who wished it some spiritual guidance. One sat at the family table for meals with the licensee, his wife, and the lady guest.

Having some time on my hands before dinner, I took a walk with camera in hand among the dumps, taking some pictures. I encountered a man and his wife, their car nearby. They were noodling dumps, but they had no opal. They said that once in a while they did find an odd piece or a fragment that had been missed. But to me it appeared not worth while; those dumps showed absolutely nothing, not even a fragment of potch, for the miners did not overlook a thing. It was a needle-in-the-haystack proposition.

After dinner things really got started. Jim opened the small bar, which held a couple dozen miners and locals also. One of the most outstanding Australian traditions is beer drinking. It was not long before the bar filled up with miners after their day's toil. I was soon to be acquainted with as fine a bunch of rough-and-ready men as it has ever been my experience to meet. As the law at this particular period in the state of New South Wales was that all bars closed at 6 P.M., at about 10 P.M. I asked Jim how come he could stay open. How about the law? Jim said he was the publican, the law, and the all-around counselor. This really seemed to be the case. Those lads just drank beer, beer, and more beer. Outside on the porch of the hotel were stacked up at least fifty empty kegs, awaiting shipment back to Sydney for more beer. Everyone was engaged in the beer drinking except the lady author. Anyway, ladies do not enter men's public bars in Australia. This is out. But she could have had service in the parlor, which is the custom for ladies and their escorts.

When the miners discovered (which did not take very long to discover) that I was not an income-tax collector, everyone was my friend. When they learned that I was interested in opal and its mining, I received so many invitations to visit with them that I would be there yet if I had accepted them all.

I did accept a gracious invitation to meet the next morning with Luke Kite. Luke was on time, and, boarding his car, we drove out to the Nine Mile, where Luke's son Shirl and his two brothers Bill and Foley were waiting to greet us. As it was lunchtime, a fine meal was all ready to be served. After lunch we went to the shaft that was being sunk only a few feet distant. I learned that Luke and his son Shirl were both killing time awaiting sheep-shearing time, since both were expert sheep shearers who made as much as $40 a day each. Bill and Foley, being pensioners, stuck to the business of opal mining. I had the occasion also to visit many of the other miners and their claims, some at what is known as the Three Mile and some others farther west out at what is known as the Grawon.

Several weeks went by far too quickly, and it is truthful to say that it was with much regret that I had to depart from my new-found friends, with the promise to return some day. This I hope to do. One of the locals driving to Walgett was glad to have me accompany him. At Walgett I caught the late-afternoon train back to Sydney.

Australian trains are similar to those in Europe in that they are made up of compartments. It was after dark when one of the chaps in my compartment stated that in a few minutes we would be coming into Narrabri. "What's there?" I asked. He said: "We will all get a beer." When the train stopped, out rushed everyone, leaving a long line of open doors all the way along the platform. Everyone dashed into a large bar in the station to quench his enormous thirst.

The train started up again. The man, scanning his schedule, said: "About 1 A.M. we will come to Werris Creek." I, of course, asked: "What's there?" He said: "We get some more beer." The same thing happened as at Narrabri. Then off we went once more. The man said: "Next we come into Muswellbrook." By now I was used to the custom, and I said: "We get some more beer." "You are right, son," said he. So, regardless of what station we stopped at or what time of night it was, the train waited long enough for everyone to quench his never-ending thirst. There is an old saying, "When in Rome, do as the Romans do." So I had to do as the Aussies do and quench my thirst also. Next morning the train arrived in Sydney—a good bath and city clothes again. Then I was again on my way to visit with my city opal dealers, all of whom I know from my many past visits.

20 Australian Journeys

BEING a dealer in opal, I decided to make a trip to Australia in 1953. This trip was made after an absence of many years, for the last time I had seen Australia was during the First World War, when I had made several visits to that country. In 1953 I was amazed at the great progress toward modernism that was taking place. Where slums and early-day buildings had stood, now skyscrapers were to be seen. My trip in 1953 was by plane (Canadian Pacific Airlines) from Vancouver, with one-day stops in Honolulu and the Fiji Islands. These stops afforded some wonderful sight-seeing adventures.

My next trip, the following year, was also via plane (Pan American World Airways) from San Francisco. But this time there were no stopovers anywhere. The only difference in route was that after refueling at Nandi, in the Fiji Islands, we flew on to Auckland, New Zealand, before heading for Sydney.

The reason for my flying was more or less that of curiosity: to have the experience of that mode of travel. However, never having been in the habit of rush, push, or shove, the next year I decided to travel to Sydney via the Orient Lines' fine large liner, the *Orcades*, from San Francisco. This was a very enjoyable trip. With nearly 1,500 passengers on board, the time passed very quickly indeed, and it was no time at all till we were in Honolulu, where we spent a whole day. Our next stop was Suva, in the Fiji Islands. We always arrived early in the morning, and the whole day was spent in local sight-seeing.

The *Orcades* being a very fast ship, the 1,150 miles on to Auckland was covered in a short time. A whole day was spent looking over as grand a patch of scenery as I have seen anywhere. Sailing at midnight, we soon left the 1,280 miles to Sydney behind. On my trip the following year, since I had had such a grand time on the *Orcades*, I decided this time to travel via the *Orsova*, at that time the flagship of the same Orient Lines, departing also from San Francisco.

It had been my mission not only to purchase opal but also to visit those opal fields that were accessible—to see at first hand what the country was like, how the people and the miners lived, and how they mined and sold their opal. On my first visit, I stayed in Australia for five months. During this period I made the acquaintance of many opal cutters and, of course, met some of the most important dealers in opal. So, after these four trips to the land down under, having each time met these people engaged in the mining and trading of opal and having observed every aspect of their trade, I considered that I had really obtained an education. For one thing, I observed a great many things that were not widely known or generally understood. While in Sydney, for instance, I visited the three large museums where opal is on grand display—opal the like of which is to be seen nowhere else in the world. I met the various curators, and since I was of course also interested in mineralogy, the conversation did not always turn upon the question of opal. I had, of course, always known that Australia was a rich country noted for its mineral wealth, producing millions yearly in a great variety of mineral output, from coal to gold; and the thousands of fine mineral specimens on display in these museums attest to that. The National Museum in Sydney has a full coverage not only of the nation's mineral wealth but also of other natural objects and of many historical ones as well. At this museum I met Mr. Chambers, the able curator of mineralogy, and since I had with me a few rare mineral specimens from the United States, he co-operated with some fine exchanges.

Another excellent museum is the Mining Museum, which very probably is one of the best of its particular type in the world. It is unfortunate that this museum, which was established in the early days, is situated in a very poor locality. Because of this, I found very few visitors there; every time I went there to view the grand exhibits I was alone. There is no doubt, however, that a great many Americans interested in gems and minerals would be thrilled by a visit to the Technical Museum. In this fine institution, some early-day discoveries of opal are on display in the famous Percy Marks collection. On inquiry, I was informed that the late Percy Marks was one of the outstanding buyers of opal in the fields in the early days: those days of the great discoveries at Lightning Ridge and at White Cliffs in New South Wales. In his day, the present fields at Andamooka and Coober Pedy in South Australia had not yet been discovered.

However, his collection here at this museum is without doubt the world's very finest. He evidently had the foresight to save some of the outstanding specimens for his collection, and therefore not all of the grand pieces went to the lapidary to be cut into gems. Today his descendants still deal in opal and operate one of the most distinguished jewelry stores on Castlereagh Street in Sydney.

It has been my pleasure to view and visit this store. Here one can purchase the finest of opals, always mounted in solid gold, and some which run into thousands of dollars. Any visitor to Australia should make it a point to visit both the Percy Marks collection displayed at the museum and the Percy Marks jewelry store. As we have noted in another paragraph, one need not have any qualms in regard to fakes, glass imitations, or even synthetics of any kind. For every item, regardless whether it be opal, emerald, ruby, or sapphire, is genuine, and of the finest quality.

As a postscript to this account of my visits to Australia, I should like to add the following item.

A Sydney gem merchant recently slept in his locked pickup truck with a loaded revolver at his side while on his way from Sydney to Adelaide with opals expected to bring as high as $75,000. He was my good friend E. Gregory Sherman of Pymble, a suburb of Sydney. His parcel included a 38-ounce solid opal, the largest stone ever found in the field. The total contents of the parcel amounted to 300 ounces, including the world's largest opal matrix. Opal matrix includes the opal associated with quartzite which was originally sand and is now metamorphosed. It usually holds a large kernel of precious gem opal. Otherwise it is sold for its specimen value.

Having bought the opal, Mr. Sherman decided for safety to keep his route to Sydney somewhat secret. He kept away from hotels each night and parked in the bush off the roadside. "I wasn't taking any chances," he said. His opals traveled wrapped in blankets, hessian sacking, and an eiderdown quilt and rode on top of an old inner tube to cushion any shock from the rough road.

Mr. Sherman stated that he paid $17,000 for the gems but estimated them to be worth close to $75,000—that is, after cutting, polishing, labor, and of course sales tax. The 38-ounce opal and the specimens with matrix would all be retained in one piece to enhance their value as collectors' or museum pieces.

Mr. Sherman reported that their discovery was made by sheer luck. A lubra (aboriginal woman) was digging in an abandoned opal shaft in the field. The rubble from the pit became too hard for her to lift out, so she asked a male aboriginal for help. He in turn obtained two more natives to help him with the work. The first man was the one who actually discovered the big gem.

After they had been paid, two of the natives went to Port Augusta to buy a new pickup truck with their shares. One of them went on a terrific bender and landed in jail. The third fellow was flat broke after two nights of gambling. Mr. Sherman stated that he had paid the natives several thousand pounds for their opal and matrix specimens, the pound being equal to $2.24 in American money at the time. A recent press release stated that the large gem was shipped to New York, where a buyer paid $70,000 for it.

21 Wollaston's Journey for Opal

THIS CHAPTER is devoted entirely to T. C. (Tully) Wollaston's account of his journey with his partner, Herbert Buttfield, from Adelaide in the state of South Australia to the Kyabra Hills in southwestern Queensland in search of opal. This journey covered more than 700 miles through practically unknown country. The Wollaston account came into the possession of the author, and it is reproduced here for the first time. The reader will no doubt be at a loss to comprehend some of the text fully, since some words used by Wollaston are those used in the Australian outback, but the story is related here exactly as Wollaston wrote it. The reader will also chuckle at some of the events he describes. At the same time the narrative of this journey will give the reader a fine character analysis of the man in all respects. He was a great Australian, an outstanding man, and a true leader.

§ Off to the Opal Country

Thus it came about that, struggling out of the backwash of the Silver Boom, and after preliminary canters in the stone line with Australian "rubies" and Tasmanian sapphires, I found myself one hot Wednesday, November 21st, 1888, heading out to "spot" Joe Bridle and his newly found opal mine on the burning ridges of the far Kyabra Hills. And one of the whitest bushmen that ever boiled a billy went with me. The programme was to hire camels from Hergott; strike across to Strelecki and on through Innamincka and up the Cooper River to Windorah, and thence through Hammond Downs, Maroo, and Tallyho to Kyabra Hills, where my meagre information fixed the man who was supposed to have made a discovery of sandstone opal. My informant had seen him there three years before, fumbling around, and that was the nearest I could get. It seemed rather a long shot, but when I closed my eyes I could see Miss Em shake her oily ringlets and point with a long decisive finger toward the North Pole. That was enough for me, and I breezed off—leaving with a pang for my young wife and a babe of six weeks old.

November 21st: Nothing worthy of note the first day but the grill at Riverton and the pretty township of Quorn circled by the Flinders Range. 111° in the shade.

November 22nd: Flinders Range is a bold and picturesque line of hills which escorts the train for several miles and divides at Hookina. (The Range opposite Mern Merna reminds one of the Marble Range, Port Lincoln side.) Saltbush country with stunted black-oak sparsely distributed, and gums tracing any creeks.

Good old "gibbers" soon began—the unmistakable hallmark of the Never-Never. These are hard siliceous stones like beach pebbles, smoothed by weathering and normally about the size of a man's fist. They pave the tablelands of the interior for hundreds of miles, and form the chief feature of the landscape—there is, in fact, often nothing else to form it.

November 23rd: Hergott. Red clay plain, treeless and grassless. Stock dying everywhere. About 100 a week being dragged away from the bore and burnt. Found we had overshot the mark, returned to Farina and arranged with Mr. Richardson for two riding camels as far as Innamincka. There a third would be available for Tomtit, our black boy, out of a loading pack then due to start with Abernethy in charge.

November 25th, Sunday: I had a poor kick-off. Buttfield,

my mate, suggested I should save two days' travelling with camels and go out as far as Lyndhurst with a station-hand in a trap. I fell in with the idea—and that was only the beginning of the descent. The driver was in that affectionate stage of drunkenness when he is apt to repose on one's bosom and croon a lullaby. The road led through deep red sand across desolate saltbush plains, and I felt I couldn't stand lullabies long under such conditions; but as a discipline for the coming trip I suffered them longer than I now like to recall, till at last I had to bump Jehu off his perch and take the reins and whip, for in striking at the horses he generally missed and hit me. The night closed in very dark, the road was heavy, and a fierce hot wind stung us with sand and grit—sometimes we were on the road, what there was of it —sometimes upended on a barb-wire fence; but my companion had no preferences. He waved his oozy, damp arms and waggled his foolish head at Venus when she looked out now and then from the murky clouds, for, like Teufelsdröckh, he "sat above it all"—he was alone with the "three stars" of his spree.

It was not an auspicious opening for me, but in the early morning I got two hours' sleep on the cart-seat and then went up to the station for breakfast, where Mr. Ive and old friend Jack Bishop gave me a welcome.

November 27th: The twenty-two packs came up and at 1:45 P.M. we ambled off. This was my first experience of camel, but I felt quite at home behind that lofty summit, rather to my surprise. The Australian rides behind the hump on a wooden framed saddle and not on the apex as in the East. It is further from the treacle-like juice that oozes from the back of the beast's neck, and one cannot be scraped off quite so easily if the deft animal dodges under a straggling limb of timber—it hits the hump first.

At five miles, Frome Creek; silver-grey wattle, titree,

and eucalyptus traverse its main bed. Sharp abrupt ridges of red slate—the scattered tiles lying in all directions. Picturesque country. Rock wallaby and kangaroo abound.

November 29th: Made Freeling about 3 P.M. and Old Freeling at sunset. Pretty spot; hills higher with mulga, cotton bush, broom, and eucalyptus; two huts in the valley.

November 30th: Coolest day since leaving Adelaide. Camped mid-day at TrinityWell. But at one o'clock a furious gale arose and blew with incredible force all afternoon and night, bringing from the camping grounds—a central watering place—suffocating clouds of dust.

December 1st: Made twenty miles by 2 P.M. and reached Blanchewater, a chain of large pools or miniature lakes of fresh water, with sloping banks thirty feet high. The largest one is about half a mile long, six to twenty feet deep, and abounds with fish. Ducks, shags, cranes, ibises, and water hens are plentiful, and the iarge gums [eucalyptus] that border the waters are white with cockatoos, the nature of whose shrill din suggests an hilarious attempt to justify a base deed. Snipe and spoonbills wade round the clumps of very fine green bulrushes; the rock wallaby threads his way amongst the miniature crags, leans out at odd angles from crevices and small fantastic caves; and now and then a brilliant blue kingfisher flits across from bank to bank or darts into the clear waters to claim his share of the spoil.

A pretty picture, surely, yet lying dead and dying along the track and near these very water holes are scores of cattle, sheep, and horses. A perfect paradise for birds, and wallabies can dig out roots of all descriptions and top-up with bark and gum nuts, and hither these favoured ones are drawn in drought time when their local sources fail; but the larger animals, alas, grow weaker and weaker as they nose over the foodless plains and at last hug the waters and starve there while the birds and furry night-beasts delight their little souls in fatness. It seems a horrid arrangement, but is mainly due to man's want of foresight and conscience.

Spelled here all next day, and shot teal and wood-duck and devoured them, and varied the menu with fish. Glorious swim night and morning. Washed my moleskins and praised God.

December 3rd: Lunched at Blanchewater station [ranch], three miles further on, and, before leaving, George Clark cut my hair with the horse clippers.

December 4th: Deadly day. Twenty-five miles of fierce sun, sandhill, and shadeless plain. Reached Monte Collina at 4 P.M. Horses, sheep, and even crows dead round the well and others dying; water salt and putrid.

December 5th: Short stages, ten miles; struck Strelecki Creek; also ants, wasps, and flies in myriads. Flocks of gelars [a parrot] first noted here, and thence onward all over Western Queensland. Dear, friendly birds.

December 6th: Passed Caraweena Station, but did not call. Camped at Sawpits. Saw the first bauhinia tree today, which is plentiful further on; a large-framed tree with thick dark-green foliage, leaves not unlike the Judas tree. The long pods contain beans said to be nourishing, but we were content to let the camels decide it.

December 7th: Two baby camels made their appearance during the night, and we spelled the day to give them an opportunity to unwind their legs. Next day they rode aloft on the maternal humps. Odd little fellows. Heat almost unbearable.

December 8th: Horrible to see stock dying everywhere, to hear their loud harsh breathing and watch their patient misery. It stabs me to the heart with a kind of rebellious wrath. Who is responsible? It seems so callously wicked that to be accompanied with this daily awful horror lies on my spirits like a suffocating shadow. We killed some sheep today with a tomahawk to end their sufferings. The air is tainted for miles, and the whole country is a roasting Gehenna.

December 9th: Heat unbearable, close, and stifling; mosquitoes and ants beyond belief. Heavy dust storm broke over us; lurid clouds, but no rain fell. At 4 P.M. moved on to Tinga Tingana, known as Burkitt's; made heartily welcome and stayed that night.

December 10th: Mrs. Burkitt, secret disciple of Miss Em's, has a collection of agates and pebbles from the Strelecki. To have a chat and break camel monotony was refreshing. Pushed on seven miles after lunch, and camped at well in the creek bed.

December 11th: Waiting for packs all day—they contained the food. (I miss my sweetheart very much.) The birds are very tame, through the parching heat—greenies, mynahs, crested pigeons (wongas), and zebra finches come down and drink from a jam tin I have filled from my bag. One little bird, a sweet grey-green little thing, rather bigger than a silver eye, came into Burkitt's tent where I was lying and sat on my chest and then on my face. I caught it and gave it a drink, but after I let it go out it returned several times and would sit on my finger like a tame bird, which I thought very strange.

December 12th: Arrived at Toolache about 3:30 P.M. 118° in the shade, with furious hot wind blowing. Tommy Rough, renowned far and wide for his profanity, is the presiding genius here—a kindly soul, interested (God help him) in his garden and his fowls, and not to be judged by his wild tongue, which seems perhaps but a natural product of this unrelieved expanse of red-hot desolation. Dust storms throughout the night and a few drops of hot rain—

then stretches of suffocating closeness, with mosquitoes as large as bees. The nights are awful.

December 13th: Some solid comforts, including the water (got ancient 'possum's leg in my billy at first dip). Ground thick with tiny burrs which our nap takes up and retains for our delectation during the day (we ride on our nap on a wooden saddle).

December 14th: Innamincka at last. Only twenty-three days since leaving Adelaide, and its has seemed like twenty-three years. Bought a watermelon from John Chinaman—God prosper him!

December 15th & 16th: Letter writing, playing chess with the trooper, and swimming in the Cooper.

§ Innamincka to Windorah

December 17th: Ordering stores and getting ready for the start, which we began at 5:30 P.M., and made twelve miles by moonlight, passing Koonamurra water hole, largest on the Cooper, which abounds with fish and game.

December 18th: Made Nappamerry about 4 P.M. Met Mr. Conrick, the owner, who made us welcome and prevailed on us to stay. Good stone house and outbuildings. What an oasis! Glorious fresh-water lake, rock-bordered and tree-girt. Swans, ibises, ducks, and waterfowl of all descriptions foregather here, and Conrick allows no shooting near the station. Fine fish abound in the lake, and we swam after them for hours but caught none.

December 19th: Swim at 6. Cooler today, but bad going—sand and porcupine. "St. John," my riding camel, fell with me three times today. Reached water hole 7 P.M., tired out—aching limbs and sore throat. The hills, called St. Anns, have curious rounded tops and are of even height.

December 20th: Made Barioola by 3:30. Very tired and unwell.

December 21st: Travelled through Mulga today, and "dead finish," a straggling crooked acacia (wattle) : needle-like foliage and fine dark red wood. Excellent pipes are made from the fragrant root wood, but the upper wood cracks. A wonderful change has come over the country since yesterday. Fairly timbered and any amount of good dry feed; tussock and Mitchell grass. "Caustic" is a curious growth—up to two feet high, like light-green macaroni or rounded sea-grass, the stems full of acrid milk—I do not know the botanical name. Bad road; gibbers all the way. Camel tender, and I walked ten miles on foot.

December 22nd: Horrible day. Gibbers, flies, and tender-footed camel. Twenty-two miles. Camped in dry water-course. Caught trumpeter for supper in a waterhole. As I fished, a pretty banded water rat whisked about all the time —I nearly hooked him. Early next morning he was there again, diving and fussing around, and finally climbed up on a dry tree trunk that stretched from the opposite bank well into the pool. There he dolled himself up, curled his whiskers, massaged his pink nose, drained the water out of his back hair, and let the early morning sun soak into his ribs— the one blessed hour for man as well as rat: 4:30 to 5:30 A.M., fly-free, sometimes cool, usually still, bracing one to endure the shadeless horror of the gibber plain. Presently I espied a large grey wildcat stealthily emerging from the stunted bluebush on the opposite bank. Puss had been on the same enterprise before, and was coming on spec, as the rat was not visible to her. I petrified myself and rod so well that she did not spot me at all, although in full view. She crept down the bank and then paused at the butt of a fallen tree. I heard the softest "pop" like a bream lazing up, and there was ratto yards away under the water, the chuckling brat. He also had been at the game before. Blissfully unconscious, puss crept warily forward, stealthily flattened her body along the log, moving like a huge grey caterpillar, but so deadly in earnest, so tragic even. "Old Stripey" was coming back again in open derision, with the tip of his red nose making rings on the water, and the silent drama tickled me immensely. The cool insolence displayed by the hunted one, blowing out as he did small beady bubbles now and then, accompanied by scornful little sniffs as he came nearer, made me rejoice so incautiously that I rang down the curtain all too soon, and puss, pausing for one agonised instant, dashed off, a mere streak of grey fur, into the saltbush. How often had the game been played, I wondered. And would "Old Stripey" fall a victim at last, and his humorous pink nose pay the penalty of its impudence? I fervently hoped not. At any rate, I was cheered all that day to think that in the "Lives of the Hunted" there was one that managed to extract a good bit of fun out of the business. Passed Durham Downs today —a well known station.

December 23rd: Same old conditions; sore-footed camel; walked ten miles on foot. Mirages wonderful today; unbelievable till seen. We sing by turns every song we know to cheer each other on. The hours drag out so interminably we dare not look at our watches. The first semblance of shade near noontime we usually embrace as the signal to camp for our mid-day spell; one withstands during the morning numberless assaults of "craving-to-see-the-time," and then, finally succumbing in the blessed hope of indicated noon, finds perhaps 8:45 A.M. registered: to "wait for the morning watch"—yes, I feel I know all about it.

December 24th: Padded out 25 miles today; passed Tarco Station about one mile and camped at Tarco waterhole. Had a glorious swim. Fifty to sixty blacks were here netting fish.

Like birds and wild animals they draw in to their blessed lands of Goshen in times of drought and trouble, and it's man's greed and carelessness and callousness surely which together are responsible for the wholesale starvation of animals introduced. We destroy their instincts, ring-fence them, and let them depend on our catering—and our catering amounts to a few dams—and damns.

We exchanged some flour and tobacco for seven large "Emperor" fish weighing from 2 to 5 lbs. each, and we tried to eat the lot, as the weather was horribly sultry and we could not bear to think of wasting such celestial food. We had to give in before we got half through. The trumpeters I catch here and there at the waterholes are mere vexatious playthings, full of sharp bones, and only serve to tease one back to a lusty bite of tinned meat.

Whether we ate too much Emperor, as seems likely, or whether the awful oppression of a brooding thunderstorm was responsible, or both, we spent a racking night—devoured by mosquitoes, persecuted by burrs, and waiting for the burst of rain which never came.

December 25th (Christmas Day): Long, wearying day, oppressively hot—camels slow and weak. Camped in an old dry donga for lunch and pledged our wives in cocoa. More than once we casually alluded to the fact that we had "something stronger in the pack," and though we did not openly say so, I think we were both rather impressed with the unusual character of our self-restraint. For be it realised the sun had been boring into our necks for five solid hours, and the lunch that fell to our lot that day was damper [a sourdough type of bread] and tinned cow's heel, jolted into a warm gluey liquid with froth on it.

If either had given a lead—as we both, it seems, had secretly prayed—solid support would have been accorded by the other, for on later reflection we came to the conclusion that, having gone so far as to have "something stronger in the pack," it was an error of judgement on such an occasion to leave it there. But we often benefit by our errors, and it is comforting to think that this may have been one of them, for it took rather more moral courage than we could well spare to attack those freckled islands of cow's heel, lying in their frothy sea of glue—that is, in the true joyous Christmas spirit. A tot of Usher [a brand of Scotch] might have put a bead on our gratitude.

December 26th: Made Gilpippie—ten miles. Heat intense; couldn't face it, and camped till 4 P.M. Pretty country just here, grassy flats and small red sandhills with bushes, clumps of gum trees, and bauhinias.

December 27th: Same old entry: "heat awful." Self and beast utterly tired on reaching Tanbar at 9:30 P.M. The sun went down rayless in an angry murk of blood, and a hot wind came fanning over the stony floor. I was desperately tired; partly delirious, perhaps, for I seemed to be laughing or crying at intervals or talking to myself. Buttfield had gone ahead to pick a camp; his camel was much stronger, but my poor beast I had had to urge all day to make him travel at all, and had walked on foot as long as I could hold out. I shall, as long as I live, remember that blood-red sun sinking over the blackening desert, that sickening hot wind, fanning up as it were from Gehenna, the smell of smoking clay and burnt stones, and the sinking sense of despair. I was cold and clammy. I crouched on the saddle and tried to pray for strength to hang on, but nothing but meaningless words seemed to come—some of them approached the humorous indeed, as when I found myself repeating "bless the porcupine with understanding." It was really a very fine original prayer—requiring much faith—but I didn't know it then. I repeated the words again and again till I got a gleam of business sense which braced me up a bit. "You're going miffy at the top, lad," I said aloud, and, looking up from my crouching position, I could see that patient old head held wearily aloft plodding painfully along, and a thrill of compassion set my blood humming again. I could have hugged the old darling if he had been more adaptable for the purpose. As it was, I called to him to breeze along and hang it out, and I would pledge my honour he should have a week's spell at Tanbar.

December 28th, at Tanbar Station: Tanbar—a fine name, and fine people. The Hendersons were very good to us, invited us to breakfast and dinner, and loaded us with good things when we left at 2:30. Tanbar and Nappamerry stand out like lighthouses on our chart. True to my promise I left old St. John at Tanbar with Tomtit, the native boy, to follow on later, when both had spelled a bit, and I took Bulby, the black boy's camel. It was a good exchange, and the rest and good food of the day helped me very much, and we camped again, and had a long night and good sleep at the Nine Mile.

December 29th: Early start. Made thirty miles, our record, I believe, to date, reaching Witcherloo, an out-station of Tanbar, at five o'clock. Meals at hut; usual salt junk. Hard days, but I was young and pretty tough. Met a big, burly fellow here with exceedingly dirty white shirt front, but with a large diamond stud.

December 30th: Hot, wearisome day. Reached Stony Point (Windorah) at five. The whole township came out to spy on the camels and criticise their odour and anatomy—both unknown there before. The blacks call the camel *emunando* —i.e., "emu-horse," which is pretty cute, I think.

December 31st: Dreary hole. Township *en fête.* Races— beastly hole at any time I should say; super-beastly at racetime, as I can vouch. The boisterous hilarity of drunken men, or semi-drunken men, is wearisome and disgusting anywhere, but New Year's Eve humour, especially in an outback township where races have drawn the crooks and spielers together for miles around, is a special type. It is difficult to get far from the madding crowd, because there is only scrub or spinifex about, and the crowd straggles along too. If you sit down, the burrs stick and the ants bite you.

We knew we should receive marked attention later on when the fun grew fast and furious, being strangers, and we made our preparations. We first made a doss out amongst the spinifex on the rise beyond any buildings—spinifex, like adversity, keeps people off. Then we mixed with a riotous horde till towards midnight and had a parting glass, ostentatiously led out the stray goats that usually accumulate under one's bunk in these parts, and muddled our beds (as the children say) to show we were using them—which we weren't. Then, extinguishing the light, we slipped through the back window into the back yard, ducking under buckboards and over piles of bottles on all fours, and through a green drain.

We waited in the shadow of the pigsty, and peered out listening from that savoury vantage point to make sure the coast was clear. High-pitched wailing, as of exceedingly lost chords, it came floating on the rum-scented night breeze. It was the "moaning of the bar," and we took courage and faded off into the pale night.

It was better than being glued to a gin-case and stuck on the counter, "shouting" [buying] for all hands and listening to their dulcet strains. We had scarcely laid aside the last pipe—"sweetest of the day"—and settled into the soft sand, when the storm broke and the stream of muddled, maniac humanity, with tins and pots and bullock bells and flaring torches, came climbing out of the landscape, and we could plainly see them concentrate on the back room which had been ours. They were baffled there, and so began the hunt, and we thought the surging mob were surely on our trail. With wild whoops, cat calls and dingo [native dog] howls they made straight for our camp, seeming much nearer than they actually were by the flaming torch-light. But on the way they chanced on some hapless humpy not yet molested and where a quiet family lived. Them, with horrible yells and jangling, they furiously baited, hammering on the door and threatening to pull Jock out of bed feet foremost, and his missus too, unless he skipped up quick and lively and "shouted" for the crowd.

But a lusty mother had been trained in quite another school, and with disconcerting alacrity she emerged quicker than they had bargained for. "Hot water you've got inside," she exclaimed, "now try some outside." And with a deft swing of a big washing dish she soused the scalps and upturned gibbering faces of the crowd with a generous measure of scalding suds which had been ready on the fire. That was her idea of humour just then, and a good deal can be said for her point of view. At any rate it diverted the crowd, and we blessed her as we settled down in peace.

§ The Drought Breaks

January 1st: Telegram from home. All well with wife and babe. What a transformation! Windorah "Royal" had suddenly become the Ritz, the green sluggish drain was the Danube, or the Rhine at Schaffhausen; the rank old billy-goat a saintly Mahatma. It really shows it's the way we look at things that counts—and Ruskin, you remember, recommends anyone grown stale with sight-seeing to hang the head down and look between his legs in order to appraise the true value of the landscape. Races (and fights) all day.

January 2nd: More races—and more fights. The crowd would leave the races to see the fights, and vice versa, and there was general disintegration—and enjoyment. But we felt it was a time for self-discipline, so we hooked up the camels off the roly-poly* and pushed out at 5:30, consoled by the reflection that we might strike better places, but couldn't strike worse.

We had not gone far before a sharp thunderstorm broke over us, and then—then—could it be possible?—steady rain set in. The drought breaks. Gloria in excelsis!

Soaked to the skin but exultant, we swished on, singing "Oh Dinney, come out of the wet." The night was very dark, and the camels couldn't get their sea legs; they flopped about like walruses, and when we reached the Crossing, we decided to camp. It is a mud hovel at the crossing of the Cooper River, and the publican and his spouse were away at the races, of course. The "hotel" had been left in charge of a Yellow Billy [half-breed], and when a "push" came along (en route to the races) and found such an easy win, they promptly relieved the half-caste, and now lay about in all stages of argumentative, vocal, and lachrymose intoxication. It was a strange scene; any imaginative person unused to Never-Never conditions might easily have concluded that he was on the Ark, and that Noah was wetting the new baby's head, and had invited the menagerie to join in—for dogs, goats, cats, fowls, and a few lambs were huddled inside (to get out of the rain) under the tables and bunks, in the fireplace, and in every corner, and a flaring "slush lamp" lit up the weird picture. One great hairy lout lay on the broad of his back on the bumpy mud floor singing love songs, and a wet dog was curled on his chest shivering—more perhaps at the sentiments so frankly expressed than because of the cold.

*Roly-poly is an odd bush-like growth as round as large as a pumpkin. It is prickly when dry, but camels are not fussy and munch it up. It is a curious sight to see scores of these straw-coloured grass balls bowling along the plain in a hot wind, and sometimes as they roll past, a camel will snap one up, as if trained at shortstop, and transfer it into his system as he ambles along.

The livestock did not agree too well amongst themselves —there were periods of calm and then seismic movements, and a goat would walk on one's neck or a rooster shake its wet tail in one's ear. Altogether it was rather unrestful, and we wished we had come over to reconnoitre before shooting our packs. Sleep was impossible; it was cleaner and less damp in the mud and rain, and we crept out with a welcome for both, in our relief from the strange conditions within. It should be explained that a bush "pub" of this grade is made of logs and mud and has one large space called the coffee room, from which there are apertures to bedrooms and also to the bar. There are no doors, and the floors are all clay, worn into holes. The bunks are made of bags and mulga, and the roof is thatch or iron, or both in places, or patched from any old material lying about.

There are three such "hotels" in this district to my limited knowledge—Pinthara, Tallyho, and the Crossing, and those who are responsible for granting them licences should be sentenced to live in these hovels every annual holiday they take. Animals—chiefly goats and fowls—can come into one's bedroom at any time, day or night, and do, and bunt you in the small of the back as you dream, or snore on your pillow as only a whiffing rooster can.

I had come to the conclusion already that chasing the twinkling gem was not all moss and humming birds, and I tightened my belt and put another half-hitch on my courage.

January 4th: Reached Tenham at lunch, and then pushed on to Maroo Station. Mr. and Mrs. McGeorge made us very comfortable. A poor place but fine people, and that makes the difference. Clean beds with sheets (ye gods) and food free from the multitudinous army of biting, buzzing, and crawling insects, and from burrs and sand.

January 5th: Lovely day, and we're just the boys who could prize it. "Hardship is worth while," we said.

January 6th: Got away at 2:30 and made sixteen miles. Took with us Old Stanley, whom we had dug up at Stony Point: supposed to be a crafty bushman and to know the opal country—but a poor discovery, as will later appear. Camped at pools in the lignum, where the mosquitoes and frogs made sleep impossible for themselves and us.

On the break-up of a big drought the channels and billabongs,* dongas, and gilgais,* the lignum swamps and the whole country palpitate with green frogs—and if the magicians of ancient Egypt had known of a similar patch handy they would have needed no enchantment to flood Pharaoh out with them. As I lay in a fevered agony all night long, pierced by their shrill, raucous, and rasping emanations, I thought of the dear Onk at home—the drooping willows, the clean sand, the smell of water mint, and the reed warblers in the bending canes. "Swift-flowing Mincius crowned with vocal reeds." I said the lines over and over till at last their sweet music, like some divine anaesthetic, shut out the oozy gilgai and vocal frogs.

It would hardly be impartial of me if I did not spare a line for the mosquitoes. Hereabouts they are chiefly Scotch greys with long chequered legs and a tendency to knock-knees. They twang the harp a good deal and walk about sampling with their divining rod before they put down a bore. This gives one a fair chance to speed up their circulation. But in the swampy ground it is the black, stumpy, bandy-legged little beggars, silent as Satan, that stab and burn so wickedly, and they are as the sands of the sea-shore—innumerable.

January 7th: I swapped beasts with Stanley, and rode his brumby** on to Tallyho—log-and-mud shanty, mud floors, doorless rooms.

*Larger and smaller swampy backwash or flood pools; waterholes.

**Burmby is an Australian term for a rough, country range horse.

§ The Last Lap

January 8th: After riding to Kyabra Station for missing plans, returned to Tallyho in time for lunch, and then—at last—we pushed out for Bridle's Opal Mine twenty miles west, with our immediate destiny in the hands of our weak-eyed guide. He proved to be weak-witted and weak-kneed as well, and got us very effectively bushed [lost] even before sundown, and we deposed him, and camped at dark amongst thick mulga and gibbers.

January 9th: Next morning we were moving at 4:30, and as Stanley had an iron-hoofed brumby we sent him off to strike Joe's camp, if he could, and bring back water—but more in hope of getting rid of him than in faith that he would strike anything but Tallyho.

Strange how often it occurs that those who know the risks of an enterprise and religiously warn others, themselves fail to adopt the measures they advocate. They are caught napping.

My partner Buttfield had spent most of his time in the bush, and was never tired of rating the folly of those who take chances with the water supply, but here, because we had but twenty miles to cover, we came out with one day's supply. Of course he depended on Stanley, but Stanley was about as useful to pack on as a house of cards. We were up against it. The country was far too rough for camels to travel long—in fact, owing to cracked hoofs, it was difficult to get them to travel at all—on gibbers.

We made a start, however, and before long struck a track running N.E. and S.W., and followed till we saw it was leading back to Tallyho. We agreed to unpack and hobble the camels, and make a patient search for water first, and, if successful, then on foot to run Joe to earth. This parched country soaks up rain like a sponge, especially after a long drought, and in the creek near which the track ran there was no sign of anything wet, and our hope lay in following it up till rocks came in. If unsuccessful, we must return to Tallyho for water. We planted our packs and made them snug in a clump of gidya, and continued our search. We were desperately anxious to get forward, for at Windorah and on the track onwards we had heard persistent rumours of land being pegged out for opal leases, and an idea was growing since Stanley left us stranded, that we might be tricked. We ourselves were supposed to be pastoral men on the lookout for cattle country, and when we struck a garrulous broadcaster, we rather encouraged that idea by casual inquiries as to carrying capacity and value of stations in the district.

In less than an hour I had a stroke of luck. I was working the main creek, which was bone dry, and while pausing to fill my clay pipe I caught sight of a zebra finch flitting past, and then two or three more. They were not following the creek. I noticed that, and set myself to watch and follow the direction. Zebras are thirsty little birds and good guides to water, but gelars are brass-throated. Well, I soon had their plant—a nice little rock hole up a small blind creek off the main one.

We filled our bags and canteens, returned to our depot, made tea, filled two metal canteens, and set off in good heart at about 8 A.M. We had had three or four hours' juggling already though, and the day was going to be a frizzler. But as we felt sure we would score in an hour or two, we thought we would not open any tinned meat, but would do very well on our tobacco and tea. We had a gruelling, deadly day, and I have often thought since how nearly we came to getting pocketed in a stretch of impenetrable scrub, where the same fate would have overtaken us as befell my good mate and comrade a little later on.

What put us wrong was following the fresh horse-tracks

of Joe's mate, who had been in to Tallyho a few days before to get meat. We had been advised to look out for these tracks, and when we cut them we thought we were set fair. But the wicked old lout had been "tonic'd," as they call it, and had wandered about bushed for twenty-four hours, and came into Joe's camp from the opposite direction.

We only found this out when we got there at nine o'clock that night, Buttfield retching and exhausted and too sick to eat or sleep. Seventeen hours on our feet—and twelve of them as in a fiery furnace, over the rough ground and without a bite to eat. I was young and sound, and after a splash in the soak I attacked a rough supper of salt goat and damper, and slept like a babe.

It would be too tedious for others to read a description of our vicissitudes that day—our bad and good luck—and the last four weary miles coaxing and helping my mate along in the dark. It was only by following a foot-pad for the last lap that it was possible. But now we were actually at Stony Creek Opal Mine, and there was Joe Bridle in the flesh! That was the happy fact!

We had covered over 700 miles in seven weeks in the worst year known, and over long stretches where much manoeuvring was necessary to keep even a camel alive. We had risked the whole venture on the hope of finding a man in that ungetatable spot, whom Buttfield had not heard of for two years past at least. It sounded a ridiculous enterprise, and no doubt was so described by some of my stay-at-home friends, but it succeeded and put an end to any criticism.

Good old Joe! What a fine fellow he was, and with what quiet friendliness and confidence he met us! Somewhat over middle height, square set, and as strong as a horse, he was a terrible toiler, and the determined set of his features—square jaw and "executive" nose—were lit up by a kindly blue eye. I loved the man, though he led me many a dance, and we worked together for long years.

 I must tell here a little episode connected with Joe. I visited his dear old mother in Dorset on one of my trips to England, and the good lady's happy tears compelled me to accept without demur the impossible commission of taking out a cream cheese to her wayward but beloved son. Think of it—a cream cheese from Burton Bradstock, Dorset, to Tallyho in far western Queensland. It was wrapped up in tissue paper and some dock leaves with an outer covering of tea lead, or something like that, which I supposed was vital to cream cheeses, and I kept it just so, only putting on fresh wrappers when absolutely necessary. Of course, in the Indian Ocean it melted and ran about, and enclosed some of the tissue paper and tea lead, and when I got to Adelaide it had set hard again, somewhat in the shape of Ireland. It had inlets round the edges and corrugations all over it. In fact, it was more like a mineral contour map than anything else, showing lead deposits gleaming out here and there.

 Well, I had a fearful time with it before I got it finally delivered, and all the way up the track I wouldn't own it, but only stuck at the job of pitching it back into the coach or buckboard on the sly at the last moment, when the driver or any passenger had slung it away at stopping-places. "Here's that . . . thing again!" they would exclaim, and shy it off, holding their noses and spitting, for it smelt like a dead snake.

 When we got to Eurounghella late at night Joe was in hilarious mood and did not notice the smell. I could see the loyal side of his nature was touched as, with a few appropriate words, I handed over the cheese and bade him appreciate it for his mother's sake, for he immediately fell to and made preparations, and I heard him working at it all night. His bedroom adjoined mine with only a seven-foot matchboard partition between us, so that I was often roused when a pellet of lead fell to the floor, or Joe had a fit of wheezing, which was quite unusual with him. In the morning, though Joe appeared somewhat thoughtful, there were no other traces of a banquet except odd-shaped bits of lead and little wads of tissue paper scattered over the floor.

Here were we, weary and exhausted, stretched out in Joe's camp at Stony Creek, thankful beyond words that he, as well as ourselves, was still in the land of the living and at our service.

———•◦◆◦•———

22 In Conclusion

AS MENTIONED in an earlier chapter, to cut and fashion the gem from a piece of rough opal is a very enlightening operation. For those who would indulge in this work, either as a hobby or for profit, the circumstances are indeed fortunate. But it was not always so. Up to the period of the first world war this art and operation was practically unknown in the United States. A few professional lapidaries did exist, but they were always careful to keep the operational secrets (which were not of a complex nature) to themselves.

Most of the gem stones for world trade were cut and polished at Idar-Oberstein, Germany, which was the center of this trade. For many years whole families engaged in it, but even at this relatively recent date their equipment was prehistoric in comparison with that of the present day. In olden times Chinese and Hindu lapidaries had very crude equipment. By the appearance of this equipment it must have taken the Chinese weeks and even months to fashion some of the beautiful work on jade and agate into the finished product. It is indeed marvelous to comprehend the untiring patience of these Chinese craftsmen who produced the grand works of art in jade and agate that we observe today—and to do it with such crude equipment as they had. In fact, no present-day lapidary would even attempt to produce most of their objects of art, even with our modern equipment.

It must also be remembered that in past eras lapidaries did not have access to our present-day cutting and grinding abrasives such as carborundum and crystollon. In the early days sand of various-sized grades and crushed garnet were used as abrasives. Today, with a modern diamond saw—a tool that I first originated for the work—the finished gem (even if it is agate or jade) can be completed in a very short time. It is indeed difficult for the reader to realize the tremendous advancements introduced over the last two decades.

During the period before I originated and developed the diamond saw for this work, lapidaries cut a section from the rough by the use of what was termed a mud saw. This was a copper or steel disc, and the abrasive, carborundum or crystallon, was applied wet to the work with a brush—a dirty and very slow operation. When the diamond saw was first introduced in 1934, I then had to develop a machine on which to operate it. After this was finally accomplished, a United States patent was applied for, and a basic patent with five claims was granted. This is patent number 2431469, a copy of which can be obtained from the United States Printing Office for 35 cents.

Another problem then arose. Many cutters experienced operational difficulties with the new tool, and I had to write a treatise on the technique of operation. This treatise, entitled "The Diamond Saw and Its Operation," was published by the *Lapidary Journal*, Del Mar, California, and can be obtained from the magazine for $1.20. There is no doubt that the advent of the diamond saw had much to do with the great enthusiasm the art enjoys today.

It was not until the formation of mineral and gem societies (which include the lapidary art) that the art developed to the extent that it enjoys today: the position of being the third largest hobby in the United States, with only stamp collecting and photography surpassing it. Today there exists in practically every city of any size at least one mineral and gem society. The members of these societies come from all walks of life: lawyers, doctors, tradesmen, students, Boy Scouts, and even housewives. A great many of these local societies hold annual shows at which the members exhibit their works of art. These shows are always open to the public. And there are now so many of these societies that they have formed regional federations.

The California Federation of Mineral and Gem Societies has a membership of over one hundred individual societies, and these are constantly added to. They hold their annual convention and show, with dealer participation, in one of the larger cities, attracting thousands of visitors, not only from the local population but also from among interested hobbyists who attend from every section of the United States and Canada. There exists a midwest federation with headquarters in Chicago, as well as an eastern federation in Washington, D.C. Even Texas has a federation. At these large federation shows and also at local shows, dealers in lapidary equipment and mineral specimens display their wares, and gem minerals are offered for sale. Many of these dealers also offer opal in its rough state, and the hundreds of member exhibits always display some opal—some of it unmounted and some consisting of fine gems mounted in various settings.

A great number of schools throughout the country have now instituted classes in lapidary and jewelry work, taught by efficient instructors. Many students cannot afford the high-priced gem opal and therefore use the cheaper varieties like white opal, producing attractive and even salable gem stones.

Like participants in other occupations and hobbies, the members of mineral and gem societies and the dealers in equipment and materials have their trade magazines. These magazines have national circulation and also foreign circulation, especially in Canada. One such magazine is the

Lapidary Journal, published at Del Mar, California. Another is *Gems and Minerals*, which is the official journal of the California Federation of Mineral and Gem Societies and is published monthly at Mentone, California. Then there is the *Mineralogist*, a bi-monthly also published at Mentone. *Rocks and Minerals*, published at Peekskill, New York, is the official magazine of the Eastern Federation of Mineralogical and Lapidary Societies. All these fine journals cater extensively to the hobby and art; their pages contain many advertisements of dealers who offer opal for sale: opal in finished gem stones as well as in its rough state for the cutter to fashion his own gems from.

Finally, I trust that the reader has obtained some interesting knowledge in regard to that exquisite, fascinating, and most mysterious of all gem stones, the opal. And it might well be that he may fathom some of its unsolved mysteries, which have thus far puzzled science. I also wish the reader much pleasure and satisfaction if he happens to indulge in this enchanting work, not only with opal but with other gem stones as well. Adieu.

Glossary

[NOTE] *An asterisk denotes a jewelry term.*

agate opal: This is a misnomer. It is either opal or agate, since it is mineralogically impossible for it to be both.

aranjados: Mexican term for cherry or honey opal from Querétaro

* black opal: gem opal of the darker varieties, whether green, blue, or gray. No Australian opal is true black. True black opal occurs only at the Rainbow Ridge field in Nevada.

boulder opal: colorful opal permeating and sometimes coating a silicified limonite from Quilpie, Queensland, Australia

cherry opal: dark, translucent, amber-colored opal from Querétaro, Mexico

chrysopal: another term for the mineralogical name prase opal; a green variety of common opal

common opal: mineralogical name of the mineral $SiO_2\,H_2O$, which is rather plentiful but has no significant value

dendritic opal: common opal which displays black mosslike inclusions of the mineral manganese, never evident in the gem varieties

* fire opal: a term given to precious opal displaying outstanding red colors

fluorescent opal: common opal which displays fluorescence when activated by ultraviolet light

girasol: precious opal displaying many colors; a rarely used term for fire opal

* Harlequin opal: precious opal displaying colors in tilelike patches similar to mosaic or inlay

highgrader: American term for one who steals ore from a mine

honey opal: translucent honey-colored opal from Querétaro, Mexico hyalite opal: mineralogical term for glass-clear variety of opal found in vesicular vugs or coating basalt; an igneous rock

matrix opal: opal of gem quality having its association with rock or any contact material

milk opal: white variety of opal sometimes containing pin-fire effects and sometimes colorful veinlets

moss opal: variety of common opal containing dendritic inclusions

nobbies: gem opal in almond-shaped pieces, occurring only at the Lightning Ridge field, New South Wales, Australia

noodler: one who combs opal dumps searching for any overlooked values

opal: an amorphous form of silica, hardness 5.5—6.5; chemically defined as SiO_2H_2O

opalescent, opaline: terms given to materials having the appearance or luster of opal, usually glass

opaline: *see* opalescent

opalite: not a recognized term, but used by some to describe common opal

opalized bone: mineralogically and paleontologically described as opal replacing bone (opal pseudomorph after bone)

opalized shells: same as above—opal replacing shells or marine vertebrates; famous and at one time extensive at the White Cliffs field, New South Wales, Australia

opalized wood: mineralogically described as a pseudomorph—opal replacement of wood

pineapples: name given to an opal pseudomorph—opal replacement of gypsum crystals (rare) from the White Cliffs field, New South Wales, Australia

* pin-fire opal: milk opal displaying many fine and colorful specks throughout its structure

potch: Australian term for common opal, usually mined along with gem varieties at all fields

precious opal: opal as a jewel, differentiated from common opal (potch)

pseudomorph: (literally "false form") mineral having the characteristic outward form of another species; used with "after," as in opal pseudomorph after wood rockhound: American term for amateur mineral and gem collectors, including amateur lapidaries

rough opal: opal as it is mined and before being cut and polished into gems

seam opal: opal deposited in veins

Yowah nuts: distinct variety of gem opal embedded in limonite nodules found at the Yowah homestead, Queensland, Australia

Index

agate opal, 171
Aladdin Mine, 64–65
Alexandra, Queen of England, 148
Andamooka, 29, 31, 35, 41, 51, 52, 62, 67, 74, 82, 96–108, 109, 110, 112, 116, 125, 148, 185
Anderson, Chester A., 129, 130
Archevelita, Dan, 125–26
Arizona, opal locations in, 30
Art of the Lapidary, The (Sperisen), 36, 171
Australian National Museum, 61, 184
Australian opal, 22, 24, 29, 31, 32, 40, 41, 43, 46, 51, 52, 53–69, 73–94, 96, 102–15, 137, 141, 148–49, 154, 166–67, 168, 171, 172, 174, 181, 184–87

Barnett, Charlie, 35
Berlini, Max, 82–83
Bird of Paradise (opal), 149
black opal, 23, 24, 41, 86, 87–88, 90, 93, 120–21
Blethen, Harmon, 149
Bodel, Fred, 91–92, 94, 95
Bond, Herb, 65
boulder opal, 54, 64
Bridle, Joe, 66, 67, 188, 205, 207–8
British Museum, 137, 148
Brukarz, Harry, 151–53
Butterfly (opal), 149
Buttfield, Herbert, 66–68, 188 ff

cabochon cut, 155, 162
California, opal locations in, 30, 135

California Federation of Gem and Mineral Societies, 212, 213
California State Division of Mines, 30,
California State Mineral Museum, 30
Ceskoslovensko (Hungary), 31
checking, *see* crazing
cherry opal, 132, 134, 136
Claringbull, G. F., 137
color in opals, 21, 23, 33–36, 39–45, 46, 170
common opal (potch), 21, 23, 24, 29–30, 36, 52–53, 121, 139, 167
Coober Pedy, 29, 31, 35, 62, 66, 74, 82, 109–12, 116, 125, 185
cracking, *see* crazing
crazing, 29, 45, 117, 154–55
Csermenitsa (Hungary), 22
Cunnamulla, 54, 58, 63, 69
cutting and polishing, 156–65; equipment for, 156–61
Cyschewentza (Hungary), 65

Dake, H. C., 36, 43–44, 45, 154–55
dealers, 59, 61–62, 65, 68, 82–83, 86, 88, 90, 138–40, 141, 146, 147, 148, 151–53, 185, 186–87
dendritic opal, 171
doublet (two-piece opal), 43, 46, 51, 166–69

East Bay Gem and Mineral Society (Oakland), 146
Eastern Federation of Mineralogical and Lapidary Societies, 213

Elizabeth II, Queen of England, 148
Empress Eugénie (opal), 149
Epoxy, 169
Eulo, 63, 69, 70, 74
Eulo Queen, 70–72
evaluation of opal, 61–62, 138, 147–48

Field Museum (Chicago), 148
fire opal, 23, 46, 51
flame opal, 51
Flame Queen (opal), 92–93
Flinders, James, 116
fluorescence in opals, 21, 23, 52
Foster, Mark, 35, 121–22, 125, 127–28, 130–31

gem and mineral societies, 146, 147, 211–12
gem opal, *see* precious opal
Gem Orchid (opal), 149
Gems and Minerals, 213
girasol, 171
Green, Paddy, 64–65

Harlequin opal, 23, 51
Henley, Bill, 86
history of opal as gem, 22, 31–32, 59, 63, 65, 68, 148–49
Hodson, Glen, 122, 126
Hodson, Keith, 122, 126
Honduran opal, 22–23, 135–37
Hughes, Hughie, 84–85
Hungarian opal, 22, 31, 65, 68, 136
hyalite opal, 24, 53, 136

Idaho, opal locations in, 30–31, 135
imitations, 36, 39, 45, 170

jelly opal, 42, 171
jewelers, 23, 31, 46, 51, 65, 68, 82–83, 86, 138, 140, 141, 146, 185; *see also* dealers

King Midas (opal), 149
Kite brothers, 181
Kyabra Hills, 66, 69, 74, 188, 189

Langtry, Lily, 149
Lapidary Journal, 211, 213
Light of the World (opal), 92
Lightning Ridge, 22, 23, 24, 29, 31, 52, 73–80, 115, 125, 148, 150, 172, 174–82
Lockheed, Mrs. F. H., 70, 117, 118, 120, 121, 126–28

Marks, Percy, 83, 108, 185; collection, 185
matrix, 29, 39, 51, 88
McCullum, Harry, 85
Melhase, John, 34, 35, 129
Menelik, Emperor of Ethiopia, 149
Mexican opal, 22, 24, 29, 32, 43, 45, 132–34, 136, 172; *see also* Querétaro
milk opal, 29, 41, 46, 65, 68, 137, 140–41, 170
mineralogical characteristics of opal, 21–22
Mineralogist, 36, 43, 154, 213
mining locations, 22–23, 30–32; *see also specific areas*
mining methods, 74, 79–81, 84–85, 105, 132
Mining Museum (Sydney), 115, 185
Montgomery, George, 55, 58
Morgan, J. Pierpont, 149
Murphy, E. F. (Ted), 59, 62, 68, 82, 90, 92, 108
Museum of Natural History (New York), 148

National Museum (Sydney), *see* Australian National Museum
Nettleton, Charlie, 87–88, 90–91, 93, 94, 95

Nevada, opal locations in, 22, 29, 32, 52; *see also* Rainbow Ridge
New Chum Diggings, 91–92
New South Wales, opal locations in, 22, 52; *see also* Tintinbar, White Cliffs
Newton colors, 40, 42
Nicholas II, Czar of Russia, 149
Nicols, Jack, 91
nobbies, 79, 88
opal, opals:
 color in, 21, 23, 33–36, 39–45, 46, 170
 common (potch), 21, 23, 24, 29–30, 36, 52–53, 121, 139, 167
 cutting and polishing, 156–65
 dendritic, 171
 evaluation of, 61–62, 138, 147–48
 fluorescence in, 21, 23, 52
 history of, as gem, 22, 31–32, 59, 63, 65, 68, 148–49
 imitations, 36, 39, 45, 170
 mineralogical characteristics of, 21–22
 mining locations, 22–23, 30–32
 mining methods, 74, 79–81, 84–85, 105, 132
 precious, 23, 29, 30, 31–32, 36, 39, 42, 46, 140–41, 146–47
 preservation of, 154–55
 prices of, 46, 51, 62, 82, 84, 85–86, 91, 92–93, 94, 108, 138–41, 146–48, 186, 187
 pseudomorphs, 21, 30, 53, 60–61, 171–72
 scarcity of, as gem, 23, 29, 140–41, 146
 specimen, 51–52, 54, 60–61, 117, 120–21, 122, 137
 superstitions about, 150–53
 synthesization of, *see* imitations
 trade in, 138–41, 146–48
 two-piece (doublet), 43, 46, 51, 164, 166–69
 types of, 23–24, 29, 46. 51–54
opal dirt, 79–85
Opal Shorty, 120, 121
opalite, 171
Opalton, 54, 69
Oregon, opal locations in, 30, 135

Pandora Star (opal), 91
paua shell, 43
"pineapples," 60
pin-fire opal, 23–24, 51
pipe opal, 60
potch, *see* common opal
prase opal, 23
precious opal, 23, 29, 30, 31–32, 36, 39, 42, 46, 140–41, 146–47
preservation of opals, 154–55
prices of opals, 46, 51, 62, 82, 84, 85–86, 91, 92–93, 94, 108, 138–41, 146–48, 186, 187
Pride of Australia (opal), 92
pseudomorphs, 21, 30, 53, 60–61, 171–72

Queensland, opal locations in, 22, 29, 31, 53–54, 63–69, 74, 137; *see also* Cunnamulla, Opalton, Quilpie, Yowah
Querétaro, 22, 24, 29, 31, 43, 132–34, 136, 172
Quilpie, 54, 63, 64, 69, 74

Rainbow Ridge, 22, 24, 29, 35, 41, 44, 45, 52, 53, 70, 115, 116–31
Red Emperor (opal), 92
rhyolite, 24, 29, 31, 132, 172
Rocks and Minerals, 213
Roebling, W. A., 120–21
Rogers, Austin Flint, 36

San Francisco Gem and Mineral Society, 146

Sanborn, Frank, 34
scarcity of precious opal, 23, 29, 140–41, 146
Scott, Jack, 85–86
seam opal, 109, 110
Sherman, E. Gregory, 82, 108, 186–87
Sherman, Ernie, 82, 108
Smithsonian Institution, 22, 121, 122, 136, 137, 148
Solomons, Bernie, 83
South Australia, opal locations in, 35, 41, 51; *see also* Andamooka, Coober Pedy
Southern Cross (opal), 148–49
specimen opal, 51–52, 54, 60–61, 117, 120–21, 122, 137
Sperisen, Francis, 36, 82, 171
Star of Australia (opal), 149
superstitions about opals, 150–53
Switzer, George, 22
synthesization of opals, *see* imitations

Technical Museum (Sydney), 83, 185
They Struck Opal (Murphy), 90
Tingha claim, 86

Tintinbar, 52, 112, 115
trade in opals, 138–41, 146–48; *see also* dealers, jewelers
Tweedie, Dave, 66
two-piece opal (doublet), 43, 46, 51, 164, 166–69
types of opal, 23–24, 29, 46, 51–54

United States, opal locations in, 22, 29–31, 32, 52–53, 135; *see also* Rainbow Ridge
Utah, opal locations in, 29–30, 52–53

valuators, 62, 138
Victoria, Queen of England, 148, 150
Virgin Valley (Nevada), 52, 116, 172

water in opal composition, 22, 24
White Cliffs, 22, 53, 55–62, 63, 66, 68, 71, 74, 82, 83, 87, 172, 185
Wilhelm II, Emperor of Germany, 149
Wollaston, T. C. (Tully), 31, 59, 62, 65–68, 82, 90, 172, 188–209

Yowah, 54, 63
Yowah nuts, 63–64